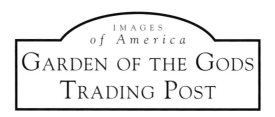

IMAGES
*of America*

# GARDEN OF THE GODS
# TRADING POST

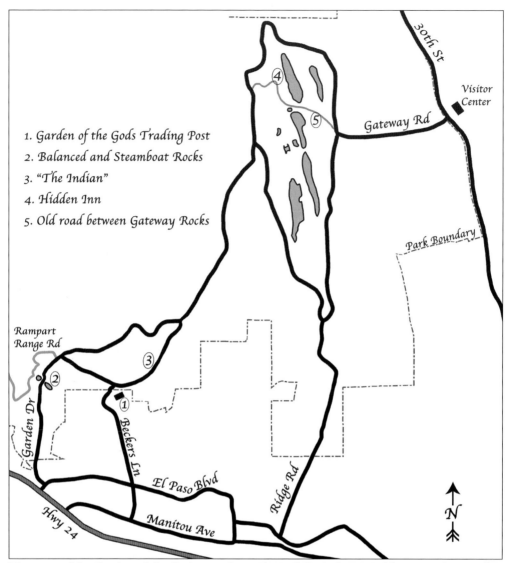

1. Garden of the Gods Trading Post
2. Balanced and Steamboat Rocks
3. "The Indian"
4. Hidden Inn
5. Old road between Gateway Rocks

*30th St*

*Visitor Center*

*Gateway Rd*

*Park Boundary*

*Rampart Range Rd*

*Garden Dr*

*Beckers Ln*

*El Paso Blvd*

*Ridge Rd*

*Manitou Ave*

*Hwy 24*

*N*

This map of the Garden of the Gods area shows the park boundaries and locations discussed in the text. (Authors' collection.)

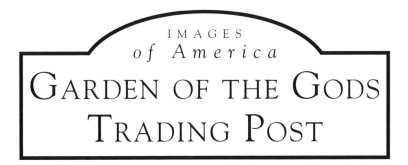

IMAGES
*of America*

# GARDEN OF THE GODS
# TRADING POST

Pat and Kim Messier
Foreword by Diana F. Pardue

ARCADIA
PUBLISHING

Published by Arcadia Publishing
Charleston, South Carolina

Printed in the United States of America

Library of Congress Control Number: 2018962700

For all general information, please contact Arcadia Publishing:
Telephone 843-853-2070
Fax 843-853-0044
E-mail sales@arcadiapublishing.com
For customer service and orders:
Toll-Free 1-888-313-2665

Visit us on the Internet at www.arcadiapublishing.com

# CONTENTS

# FOREWORD

A few years ago, on an atypical Arizona day, a light rain fell as Norman Sandfield and I traveled to Rosa's Mexican Food Restaurant in Tucson to talk with Pat and Kim Messier about the Garden of the Gods Trading Post and the silversmiths who worked there. Following lunch, Pat and Kim welcomed us to their home, where they shared information they had discovered about the various silversmiths who had worked at the trading post in the 1930s and subsequent years. We stood in their living room talking—not because our hosts did not offer chairs—but because our excited conversations kept us moving from the layout of their book *Reassessing Hallmarks of Native Southwest Jewelry* to some of the silver, copper, and aluminum items made at the trading post that they had collected. Although Norman and I were in the midst of conducting research about San Ildefonso silversmith Awa Tsireh, we were baffled by the other silversmiths who had worked at the trading post around the same time as he. Pat and Kim had learned much about these men, as well as the women who demonstrated cultural arts at the post.

In the course of researching *Reassessing Hallmarks*, Pat and Kim developed an interest in Awa Tsireh and considered writing an article for *American Indian Art Magazine*. When they learned that Norman and I were planning an exhibition and book about the artist, they decided not to proceed with the article. After Pat and Kim's book was published, and as our book *Awa Tsireh: Pueblo Painter and Metalsmith* was being designed, they inquired if we had any plans to publish something additional about the trading post as their interests had continued to grow. Pat and Kim moved forward with their plans to expand their knowledge on the topic, resulting in the book they have now written.

With their concerted efforts and diligent research, Pat and Kim have uncovered the fascinating history of Charles E. Strausenback and his Garden of the Gods Trading Post.

Diana F. Pardue
Chief Curator, Heard Museum

# ACKNOWLEDGMENTS

The authors are grateful to the individuals and institutions that have graciously helped with this project.

We are especially grateful to the Haas family and Rebekah Lang at Garden of the Gods Trading Post for their immense contributions. At Heard Museum, Diana F. Pardue, Mario Nick Klimiades, and Betty Murphy were generous with their time. Ted and Myrl Brumbaugh Hidgen shared family history about the Strausenbacks.

We thank Dianna Ayles, El Paso County Assessor's Office; Brook Cruz and Bret Tennis, Garden of the Gods Park; Stephanie Prochaska, Colorado Springs Pioneers Museum; Special Collections, Pikes Peak Library District; Melissa Lawton, Matthew Carter, and Aaron Marcus of History Colorado; Aly Jabrocki, Colorado State Archives and Public Records; Carolyn Kastner, Georgia O'Keeffe Museum; Meg Erickson, Denver Art Museum; Kelly Kilgore Chilcott; and Jonathan Batkin, Wheelwright Museum of the American Indian.

Very special thanks to Rosemary Lonewolf, who spent countless hours obtaining information about her family.

Thanks to friends who have offered encouragement over the years: Mark Bahti, Diane Dittemore, Kathleen L. Howard, Bille Hougart, Susan Schram, Congressman Doug and Jeanie Lamborn, and William Lamborn. Thank you to Pat Cattani for help with the manuscript.

Newspaper articles were accessed online at the Pikes Peak Public Library District Special Collections NewsFinder website, and the subscription sites Newspapers.com, Newspaperarchive.com, and Genealogybank.com. City directories; birth, death, marriage, and federal census records; and US Indian census rolls were all accessed at Ancestry.com.

Unless otherwise noted, all images are from the authors' collection.

# INTRODUCTION

Charles E. Strausenback was the son of a German immigrant. His father, Charley Strausenback, was born in Alsace-Lorraine and emigrated with his parents to the United States in 1850. The family settled in Illinois, but Charley wandered west and worked as a butcher on a Pacific Mail steamship or drove goats from Mexico to California, selling the butchered meat to prospectors.

By 1873, Charley Strausenback was established as a prominent cattleman in Kansas. He had 4,400 head of cattle and also ran butcher shops across the state. He and his wife, Ellen, had one daughter, Mary Ellen, known as "Minnie," born in 1882. In 1885, Strausenback owned six acres of land in Clyde, Kansas. However, in 1888, he was back on the West Coast shipping cattle from Mexico into California. Strausenback's absence seemingly left Ellen and Minnie without support, as the Clyde land was put up for auction by the sheriff in April 1890.

No records have been found concerning the relationship of Charley Strausenback and Jennie Phillips, a native of Ohio, until she gave birth to Charles E. Strausenback on September 18, 1890, in Morelia, Michoacán, Mexico. Sadly, Charley Strausenback died on July 22, 1890, and never saw the birth of his son.

After Charley's death, Jennie Strausenback returned to the United States with her son Charles and daughter Ethel, who had been born in 1880 in Kansas. Jennie made sure Charles became a naturalized US citizen in 1893.

In 1896, Jennie married Horton S. Nichols, and the family resided in Topeka, Kansas. Charles and Ethel's half-brother, Chester Nichols, was born in 1901. The marriage of Jennie and Horton was rocky early on, and in 1904, Jennie divorced Horton and was given custody of their son.

A photograph shows Charles Strausenback as a boy about 10 years old selling souvenirs in the Garden of the Gods. No documentation substantiates how he came to be in the Pikes Peak region in 1900, but that is the year he maintained was the start of his business. The 1900 US census lists the Nichols family living in Topeka, though Charles is listed as "at school." Perhaps his mother and stepfather sent the boy to live with a relative or attend boarding school in Colorado Springs.

Jennie relocated to Colorado Springs after the divorce, but Horton soon followed, and the couple was remarried on March 17, 1904. Jennie again filed for divorce in 1905, and the local newspapers reported nearly every year that Jennie filed for divorce until the Nichols family moved to Pueblo, Colorado, in 1909.

Horton Nichols died in 1913, Jennie in 1919, and Ethel in 1926; they were all buried in the same plot in Evergreen Cemetery in Colorado Springs.

Charles E. Strausenback spent the better part of his life in Garden of the Gods. Every summer as a schoolboy, he sold gypsum souvenirs near the Gateway Rocks. It was not until he was 16 and employed by the Fred Harvey Company that he worked outside of the Pikes Peak region, traveling to the Southwest to buy Indian arts and crafts. Over time, he became acquainted with the Southwest Indians and gained an appreciation for their culture and arts. In 1914, Strausenback returned to the area permanently.

His association with Curt Goerke, owner of Balanced Rock, began when Strausenback was hired to take photographs at Balanced Rock, and continued through the 1920s when he managed businesses from buildings located on the boundary of Goerke's property with Garden of the Gods park.

But it was Strausenback's relationships with and employment of Navajo and Pueblo Indians that secured his legacy. He began hiring performers and silversmiths about 1920 to work in the Garden of the Gods in the summer, entertaining tourists with dances and demonstrations of silversmithing and weaving. The Indians employed by Strausenback were very loyal, returning summer after summer, indicating that he was honest, respectful, and generous with them.

Charles Strausenback suffered a stroke and passed away on June 1, 1957, in Colorado Springs. His body was cremated, and according to his will, his ashes were scattered in the Garden of the Gods between Balanced Rock and Gateway Rocks. His widow, Esther, continued to run the trading post until her retirement in 1979, when Tim O. and Terry Haas leased the building. After Esther's death on April 7, 1995, the Haas brothers, operating as T.A.T. Enterprises, purchased the property from the estate.

In his 1954 will, Charles Strausenback bequeathed his entire estate to his wife, Esther. Since they never had children, he stipulated that in the event Esther preceded him in death, the trading post was to be donated to the City of Colorado Springs. Although the eventual outcome varied from his expectations, it is interesting to note his instructions:

> The property that the trading post I have operated for many years is located on and the rest of this tract of land is entirely unimproved and left as nature made it. The devise of this property is made under the following specific reservation and limitations: I direct that no building shall be constructed on any portion of said property, except in the immediate area where my trading post is now located, and any future remodeling or rebuilding of the trading post shall be made so as to fit with the present type of architecture of said trading post. I particularly specify that the remainder of said property shall be kept in its natural state, that no playgrounds or buildings shall be erected thereon, but it shall be kept as a natural park for the use of the public. I further direct that my estate shall install a bronze plaque on the trading post building with a suitable inscription designating that this property is given by me and my wife, Esther I. Strausenback, to the city of Colorado Springs.

Visitors step back in time upon entering the trading post where the Haas family has maintained the original vision of Charles Strausenback, conveying the ambiance of the original structure of nearly a century ago. Historic photographs of Strausenback, his Indian employees, and Garden of the Gods park decorate the walls, evoking the rich history of the building.

From left to right, Herbert, Elizabeth, and Charlotte—the children of William and Yekanasbah Goodluck—stand outside the ramada where their father made silver at the store named the Indian. On the ground are spoons and bracelets in progress along with William Goodluck's silversmithing tools. Children often participated in the making of crafts with their parents, spinning and carding the wool for their weaver mothers or operating the bellows for their silversmith fathers. This c. 1925 photograph was taken by Charles Strausenback for his series of advertising postcards.

# One

# CHANGING TIMES

To the west of Colorado Springs, at the base of Pikes Peak, lies an area of impressive red rock formations that have been known since 1859 as the Garden of the Gods. These formations have developed into one of the most popular tourist attractions in the state of Colorado.

At the end of the 19th century, Colorado Springs founder Gen. William J. Palmer and his friend Charles Elliott Perkins, president of the Chicago, Burlington & Quincy Railroad, purchased parcels of land that encompassed Garden of the Gods. Perkins left his parcels undeveloped and allowed the land to be used as a free public park.

Following the death of Perkins, his 480 acres were donated to the City of Colorado Springs in 1909. The gift included restrictions on the usage of the land: "And it shall forever be known as the Garden of the Gods, where it shall remain free to the public, where no intoxicating liquors shall be manufactured, sold, or dispensed, where no building or structure shall be erected except those necessary to properly care for, protect, and maintain the area as a public park." After the death of Palmer in 1909, his holdings around the Garden of the Gods were purchased by Colorado Springs.

From the beginning, entrepreneurs found ways to profit from the park. Semipermanent refreshment stands popped up near the Gateway Rocks, and itinerant curio dealers, such as a young Charles Strausenback, set up tripod stands or tents to sell gypsum carvings.

On January 27, 1915, an article in the *Colorado Springs Gazette* titled "Indian Pueblo Costing $6,000 Will Be New Attraction in Garden of the Gods" announced the award of the construction contract for the first permanent structure. It would be a Pueblo Indian–themed building, erected west of North Gateway Rock and hidden between two upright sandstone wedges, blending in as much as possible with the surrounding formations by being covered with red plaster.

Construction started March 16, 1915, on the three-story structure that was to include a curio store on the first floor, a tea room on the second floor, and a lookout terrace (or observatory) on the third floor. Because of its particular location, the Pueblo building was ultimately called the Hidden Inn.

Carl Balcomb, a native of Colorado Springs, was awarded the first concession. Balcomb and his wife, Kathryn, took up residence in small living quarters within the building. Balcomb added unique design elements to the building, including Pueblo-themed lighting and windowpanes made of photographic reproductions of scenes from nature, such as Mount Manitou, Balanced Rock, and the summit of Pikes Peak.

A corner of the curio room was given over to Charles Strausenback to manage the gypsum department, which consisted of his own animal carvings. According to the *Colorado Springs*

*Gazette*, "Associated with Mr. Balcomb in the concession of the inn is Charles E. Strausenback, sculptor, who has charge of the gypsum department. He has been a resident of the Garden of the Gods each year since 1900 and has spent practically all his summers there since he was a mere boy. His art objects are carved from material found near the gateway rocks and are much in demand by tourists."

The Hidden Inn opened to the public on July 1, 1915. According to the *Colorado Springs Gazette*, "The new inn has proven popular immediately and since its opening a few weeks ago thousands of visitors have already marveled at its architecture and decorations, both inside and out."

The Hidden Inn was closed at the end of February 1916, and a few weeks later, the *Colorado Springs Gazette* reported that Carl Balcomb was unable to renew the lease for the coming year. Balcomb later recalled, "The entire episode was hectic! I was too young, too inexperienced, [and] had little backing." With Balcomb unable to continue the concession for the 1916 summer season, Charles Strausenback returned to his own business ventures.

In 1919, Roy "R.S." Davis was awarded the concession and kept it through 1948. During this period, in the early to mid-1920s, Antonio Silva from Santa Clara Pueblo was hired as a greeter and entertainer for the tourists. He had previously worked for a variety of employers, including Strausenback, within the park since about 1915.

In 1948, Helen Stewart, who was at the time also the operator of Pikes Peak Summit House, took over the concession from Davis. It must have been a lucrative business, as over the next five years, Stewart invested $20,000 in improvements and fixtures to the property above the cost of the lease. She and her family ran the concession successfully until 1995, when the City of Colorado Springs decided to close the Hidden Inn to the public.

The 80-year-old building was closed because of its deteriorating condition. In 1997, it was reported that $400,000 in renovations were required to bring it up to modern safety standards. The fate of the Hidden Inn was in the hands of the Colorado Springs City Council, and as part of a decades-old plan to reinvigorate the park, the decision was made to tear down the cherished structure and replace it with natural vegetation. Demolition commenced on March 11, 1998.

1408. GATE ROCKS.

Colorado Springs was founded in 1871, and within a short time, three separate parcels surrounding the Gateway Rocks were homesteaded: the south 160 acres by James H. Hays, the north 80 acres by Sam E. Davis, and an additional 80 acres by Thomas S. Wells. None of these owners had developed their parcels, so the land had been used as a public park. Even though Gen. William J. Palmer built his private home at Glen Eyrie, he loved the garden so much that he encouraged his friend Charles Elliott Perkins to purchase the main 240 acres for $4,000 in 1879. Perkins intended to construct a home on this land but never did; instead, he continued to leave it as a free public park and purchased adjoining parcels of 80 and 160 acres in 1899, bringing his holdings to a total of 480 acres. This photograph of Gateway Rocks, published in the 1880s by William "W.A." Davis, the first curio dealer in Manitou, was taken from inside the park, looking toward the east.

In 1873, General Palmer's friend Dr. Emerions filed the homestead for 160 acres that encompassed Balanced Rock and Steamboat Rock. The land passed through many hands before coming into the possession of Paul Goerke in 1890. This photograph was taken by James Thurlow, the first resident photographer in Manitou; he arrived in 1874 and passed away on Christmas Day 1878.

Charles Strausenback had an abiding love for the Garden of the Gods, which was a frequent subject of his artwork. This print of Gateway Rocks, with Pikes Peak in the background, was his first lithograph, made in August 1938.

By the late 1890s, the Garden of the Gods was becoming a popular place for tourists and locals to take leisurely carriage rides through the scenery, enjoy picnics, or climb the rock formations. A number of entrepreneurs realized the possibilities of capitalizing on the burgeoning tourist attraction.

Semipermanent refreshment stands began to appear at the Gateway Rocks by the early 1900s. Here, a buggy is parked in front of a stand serving soft drinks, and signs advertise Orcherade and Dr. Pepper. The Perkins family gift of the land to Colorado Springs specified that "no intoxicating liquors shall be manufactured, sold, or dispensed" in the garden. (Garden of the Gods Trading Post.)

The land immediately to the east of Gateway Rocks was purchased by developers in 1886 and subdivided, establishing the town of Garden City. Edwin L. "Fatty" Rice and his wife, Phoebe, purchased some of the lots in 1892 and opened Fatty's Place, an emporium, beer hall, and curio store. General Palmer and Charles Elliott Perkins disapproved of the sale of intoxicating beverages but had little influence over Fatty's business. In an effort to create a buffer to Perkins's Garden of the Gods property, Palmer purchased the remaining Garden City lots and other parcels near the park. After Fatty's death, his widow sold the land to Palmer in 1907. Palmer ecstatically wrote to Perkins that he had purchased Fatty's property and thus became Perkins's sole neighbor on the north and east. Palmer complained that he had to pay the sum of $15,000 for the land, but that it was less than the $80,000 Phoebe had asked a few years ago. Fatty's Place burned soon after Palmer's purchase of the property. (Colorado Springs Pioneers Museum.)

White Rock is the first large formation to be seen from the eastern entrance to Garden of the Gods. As early as 1879, gypsum, a soft white stone, was mined from this formation. The gypsum was used by early entrepreneurs to fashion tourist souvenirs unique to Garden of the Gods.

A unique form of souvenir was created from the local gypsum. Fashioned into miniature figures, including books, crosses, and tree-stump toothpick holders, the phrase "Garden of the Gods" was carved into the stone while the date of purchase was added later. Alva Weeks was one carver who sold gypsum souvenirs in the park between 1904 and 1911. This bear is dated 1913, and the Billiken was created in 1910.

Charles Strausenback, a 10-year-old boy, proudly displays his gypsum carvings from a tripod stand near the Gateway Rocks in the year 1900. The ladies no doubt happily bought a souvenir of a carved book or tree-stump toothpick holder from the talented young man. (Garden of the Gods Trading Post.)

By 1909, Charles Strausenback, a young man of 19, had progressed from a tripod stand with a few gypsum carvings to a larger display. He sits, wearing a boater hat, near the Gateway Rocks with his carvings for sale, to the left of a wood kiosk. (Garden of the Gods Trading Post.)

The newly completed Hidden Inn in Garden of the Gods park, seen here on opening day, July 1, 1915, was a three-story structure. A curio store was on the first floor, a tea room and dance hall on the second floor, and an observatory on the third floor. Carl Balcomb was awarded the first concession by the Colorado Springs Park Commission.

The Hidden Inn dining room was busy on July 1, 1915, the day the attraction opened to the public. The Indian-style light fixtures and kachina andirons in the fireplace were designed by Carl Balcomb. Indian pottery, including Tesuque rain gods, line the mantle. (Photograph by Photo Craft Shop, courtesy of Special Collections, Pikes Peak Library District, 102-2007.)

This portrait of Charles Strausenback was taken about 1910. Within a few years, he would manage the gypsum department in the curio room of the Hidden Inn. A corner of the sales floor was dedicated to displaying Strausenback's animal carvings made from stones found near the Gateway Rocks in the park. (Garden of the Gods Trading Post.)

Charles Strausenback carved this book from gypsum, intended to be sold from the Hidden Inn. Carved into the cover in Strausenback's handwriting is "Garden of the Gods July 1915." Miniature stone books were popular souvenirs in Garden of the Gods and may have represented bibles.

Built west of North Gateway Rock, the Hidden Inn nestled between two upright sandstone wedges, blending in as much as possible with the formations. To cover the inn with a red plaster that matched the surrounding rocks, the park commission had a painter put samples of his colors on the rocks until they were unable to differentiate the paint from the rock.

The panorama from the lookout terrace, or observation deck, on the third floor of Hidden Inn embraces not only South Gateway Rock, Cathedral Spires, and the Three Graces rock formations, but also the interior valley of the north portion of the park. This photograph was taken by a park visitor in August 1926.

Antonio Silva, more commonly known as Jose Tafoya or Cheropee, poses at left with Vivian and Lila Mae at the Hidden Inn in 1929. Silva, a Tewa Indian from Santa Clara Pueblo, New Mexico, was hired in the early to mid-1920s as a greeter and entertainer for the tourists. Silva's Tewa name was Tsidi P'i', which means "Red Bird." He traveled with his family from New Mexico to Colorado Springs each summer to work in the Garden of the Gods. He worked at Hidden Inn for decades, retiring in 1948. Thousands of photographs were taken of "Jose Tafoya" posing with tourists.

In the shadows of North Gateway Rock, a tourist family dons Plains-style headdresses and poses with Santa Clara Pueblo Indian Antonio Silva on the porch of Hidden Inn in the mid-1920s. At this time, R.S. Davis had the concession to operate the curio store and lunchroom. The Pueblo Indian–themed building was a welcome rest stop during tours of Garden of the Gods park and remained a popular venue for decades. In 1948, Helen Stewart took over the concession and invested $20,000 on improvements and fixtures to the property. She and her family ran the concession successfully until 1995, when the City of Colorado Springs closed the 80-year-old building to the public because of deteriorating conditions. The cherished structure was demolished in 1998 and replaced with natural vegetation.

Camilio "Sunflower" Tafoya (1902–1995) from Santa Clara Pueblo was photographed on the terrace of the Hidden Inn about 1950. The son-in-law of Antonio Silva, he and his family worked for Charles Strausenback for a few years before being employed at the Hidden Inn in 1948. Camilio and his wife, Agapita Silva, became well-known potters.

Mary Grace Tafoya, Wo-Povi, better known as Grace Medicine Flower, was born in 1938 to Agapita and Camilio Tafoya at Santa Clara Pueblo. When she was young, her family came to Garden of the Gods to entertain tourists. She learned pottery from her parents and is recognized as an innovative potter for her use of the sgraffito technique to carve designs into the clay.

## Two

# THE EARLY YEARS

In 1900, when he was just 10 years old and attending school, Charles Strausenback spent his summers painting Western designs on rock slabs and carving figures from gypsum that he found in the Garden of the Gods. These he sold from a tripod stand at the side of the carriage road leading through Gateway Rocks.

As his talent grew, so did the demand for his artwork; Strausenback maintained souvenir stands in various forms at the Gateway Rocks for many summers. After graduating from school, he worked for the Fred Harvey Company as a buyer and newsagent in the Southwest before returning to the Pikes Peak region in 1914.

On April 12, 1919, Charles Strausenback married Esther Isabell Brumbaugh, who would not only become his wife, but also his business partner. Esther was born December 16, 1899, in Antrim, Pennsylvania. Her father, Walter Brumbaugh, died in 1901 when Esther was only two years old. Her mother, Anna Raymer Brumbaugh, married Hugh Ashbaugh, and the family moved to Colorado Springs in 1908.

In 1920, Charles and Esther resided in the town of Manitou, and Charles was the proprietor of a curio shop located in a wood building at the intersection of what is now Garden Lane and Beckers Lane. This land abutted the boundary of Garden of the Gods park and, at that time, was owned by Anna Becker. Signs on the building identified it as "Garden of the Gods Curio Company." To the west of the wood building was a stand where tickets could be purchased for admission to Mushroom Park and Balanced Rock, the private park owned by Curt Goerke.

One of the main attractions for Strausenback's curio businesses was a "petrified Indian" that was heavily advertised on store signage and business cards. Various signs on a number of tourist attractions that Strausenback was associated with as early as 1912 proclaimed, "Free See the Petrified Body Inside" or "Free See the Petrified Indian Inside." A number of curio stores in the Manitou and Colorado Springs area advertised petrified Indians on display; it appears there were three or four different versions. But the one Strausenback displayed—and likely carved himself—was not a real petrified body at all, but a rock statue wearing a breechcloth. This statue remained on display in Strausenback's businesses until 1979.

Strausenback's standing as a businessman was on the rise in 1920 as he became a member of the Colorado Springs Chamber of Commerce. But economic factors made an impact that year as the country was hit with a recession that lasted 18 months, and the 18th Amendment to the Constitution, informally known as Prohibition, went into effect. Tourism surely declined during this time, and many businesses suffered. Strausenback found a way to supplement his income, but it came at a cost.

Charles and Esther moved their residence to 3506 West Pikes Peak Avenue in Colorado Springs, renting from James Gregory, a local deputy. On Monday, July 25, 1921, Charles was arrested for bootlegging, and since the landlord was a deputy, the authorities needed no search warrant to enter the premises. The arrest was front-page news in the *Colorado Springs Gazette*, and El Paso County sheriff John Weir reported that in the garret of the house a large still operation was found; a truckload of accessories was also discovered. Strausenback denied that he sold any booze, declaring he made it for his own use. He said that he had found the apparatus, and that until the day of his arrest, he had considered it a good find. However, the officials also found 30 gallons of booze hidden in an old shed near a road leading to the Garden of the Gods with a well-beaten path from the still to the cache.

The *Colorado Springs Gazette* stated that the officers had known for a time that "someone in the west end was making a pretty good brand of booze." According to the newspaper article, items confiscated in the raid included one still with accessories, 40 gallons of liquor, 50 gallons of mash, a 20-gallon copper boiler, 24 bottles, 100 pounds of sugar, an oil stove, and an empty keg. Evidently, Strausenback was set up for serious business. He was charged with two counts: the manufacture of whiskey and possession of whiskey.

Two days later, Strausenback was released from the county jail on a $1,000 bond. In August, a US deputy marshal from Denver served Strausenback with a federal warrant, charging him with violating the Volstead Act. He was taken to Pueblo, Colorado, where he was released on bond following arraignment.

Strausenback pled guilty in the El Paso County Court on September 12 and was fined $200 plus court costs; however, he still stood to be tried by the government on violating federal law. He was quoted in the papers as saying, "I have learned much during the last two months," but he did not elaborate. No other records pertaining to his arrest and trial for bootlegging were found, so apparently, the federal charges were dismissed.

This photograph of Charles Strausenback on horseback was taken during his employment with the Fred Harvey Company, for which he traveled to the reservations of Arizona and New Mexico buying Indian crafts during the winters of 1906 to 1914. For a few years as a Harvey Company employee, Strausenback was also based in the Alvarado Hotel in Albuquerque as a news agent, traveling on Santa Fe trains to Los Angeles and selling Indian curios to passengers. (Garden of the Gods Trading Post.)

One of the earliest pieces of artwork by Charles Strausenback, signed "C.E.S. 1914," is a watercolor painting depicting a cowboy on a horse in a Western landscape. This painting was likely inspired by the photograph above of Strausenback on horseback. (Private collection.)

Charles Strausenback stands on the bumper of his car in Garden of the Gods. His 1917 World War I draft registration card described him as a short, slender man with grey eyes and dark hair. Even though he registered for the draft, Strausenback never served in the military. (Garden of the Gods Trading Post.)

On April 12, 1919, Charles Strausenback married Esther Isabell Brumbaugh. She was born December 16, 1899, in Antrim, Pennsylvania. When her father died in 1901, her mother remarried, and the family moved to Colorado Springs in 1908. Charles drew this portrait of Esther in 1920. (Private collection.)

As a boy, Charles Strausenback not only carved figures from gypsum but also painted on gypsum slabs. These paintings, made between 1900 and 1908, include depictions of horses, mules, and cowboys on broncs, plus rock formations in Garden of the Gods. (Kelly Kilgore Chilcott Collection, Billie Jane Baguley Library and Archives, Heard Museum, Phoenix, Arizona, RC366[1]:16.)

The most popular forms of gypsum souvenirs carved by Charles Strausenback were miniature books and tree-stump toothpick or matchstick holders. This tree stump is etched with "Garden of the Gods 1910," and the book is etched with "Garden of the Gods July 1915." Strausenback wrote with uppercase and lowercase letters on his carvings, and the date of purchase would have been etched in after each carving was sold.

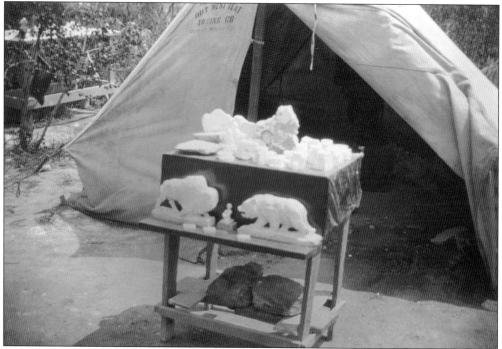

From around 1907 to 1909, Strausenback progressed from using a tripod stand to selling his gypsum carvings from a tent and table in Garden of the Gods. Some of his carvings had increased in size from small, pocket-sized souvenirs to larger statuettes. (Kelly Kilgore Chilcott Collection, Billie Jane Baguley Library and Archives, Heard Museum, Phoenix, Arizona, RC366[1]:5.)

About 1911, Strausenback erected a portable sales stand to the right of a building selling refreshments inside Garden of the Gods near Gateway Rocks. A hinged cover could be closed to protect his carvings. Strausenback probably rented space for his stand, as it was moved to various other locations until about 1915. (Garden of the Gods Trading Post.)

A view inside Strausenback's portable sales stand about 1911 shows a cash register and his gypsum carvings of bison, bears, tree stumps, books, crosses, and a female figure. As his talent grew, so did the demand for his souvenirs. (Kelly Kilgore Chilcott Collection, Billie Jane Baguley Library and Archives, Heard Museum, Phoenix, Arizona, RC366[1]:15.)

About 1912, Strausenback moved his sales stand next to a building on the east side of the Gateway Rocks. He may have rented space from Charles H. Wyman, who managed a curio shop outside the park. This location marks the first appearance of the iconic sign, "Free See the Petrified Body Inside," which became an integral part of Strausenback's business. (Garden of the Gods Trading Post.)

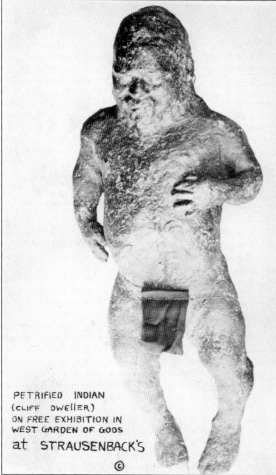

PETRIFIED INDIAN
(CLIFF DWELLER)
ON FREE EXHIBITION IN
WEST GARDEN OF GODS

at STRAUSENBACK'S
©

Tourists pose in a car in front of Garden of the Gods Curio Company in 1917. Charles Strausenback leased the wood building east of the Gateway Rocks, where he had previously had his sales stand at the side of the building. Here, Strausenback likely operated his curio business for the first time from a permanent structure.

The "petrified body" of an Indian that Strausenback advertised was actually carved from stone, likely by Strausenback himself, and was not a mummified corpse. It was small, about the size of a baby, and was on display until 1979, when Esther Strausenback retired. Although other curio stores in Manitou did display mummified remains, Strausenback respected American Indians too much to have done that.

# Three

# EIGHTH WONDER
# OF THE WORLD

The legacy of the Goerke family of Manitou Springs remains an integral part of the history of the Pikes Peak region. Paul Goerke, a German farmer, married Ida Grandt in 1876; they then sailed to the United States, disembarking in New York City in July. Finding their way to Colorado, their first son, Curt, was born in Canon City on March 23, 1877. The following year, their second son, Benno, was born. By 1879, the Goerke family was living in Rosita, Colorado, and Paul had partnered in at least four mines in Custer County. They remained in Rosita through 1885.

By 1887, the Goerkes had relocated. According to Grace Goerke Boughner, daughter of Curt Goerke, they "came to Manitou, and lived in a little stone house out near the [rock formation called] 'Old Washerwoman.' . . . Grandpa managed to get some horses and a wagon and started a freight line to Divide. My father used to help him on these trips."

In 1890, Paul Goerke obtained a lease for land north of Manitou Avenue that contained unusual rock formations, including many shaped like toadstools and two that are known as Balanced Rock and Steamboat Rock. Within two years, Goerke had contracted to purchase the land and the roadway between the two rocks from its owner, a resident of Holland.

Shortly after his father obtained Balanced Rock, Curt set up a lemonade stand near a photographer who had a picture stand at the attraction. According to Grace Boughner, the photographer "taught my father how to load the plate holders for him and eventually showed him how to take pictures. He [Curt] liked this very much and between what he could make selling lemonade and what the man paid him for helping him with the pictures, he finally earned enough money to buy the man out."

In July 1898, Paul Goerke opened Mushroom Park, a tourist attraction named after the rock formations on his land. The park was a short walk from the Manitou streetcar line on a road lined with benches and picnic spots.

By 1902, Paul had joined his son Curt in the photography business, and the company Paul Goerke & Son, Photographers, was established. They specialized in souvenir photographs of tourists posing in front of Balanced Rock, often astride burros that the Goerkes kept on the premises. They also developed Mushroom Park and built a curio store, refreshment stand, and photography studio behind Steamboat Rock.

At the turn of the 20th century, the Goerkes' photography business saw marked decreases in sales when the Eastman Kodak Company began selling portable personal cameras that made photography affordable to the general public.

Within a few years, Balanced Rock and its companion, Steamboat Rock, had become some of the most famous attractions in the Pikes Peak region. Curt Goerke advertised Balanced Rock as the "8th Wonder of the World" and proclaimed it "the most photographed object in the U.S." With the increased popularity of the park and tourists using their personal cameras to photograph the famous rocks, Curt determined the only way to continue to be profitable was to hide Balanced Rock from view and make tourists pay to see it. He maintained that all the private attractions in the Pikes Peak region were charging admission, specifically that the Hulls, the owners of South Cheyenne Canyon, were forcing the public to pay a toll to view Seven Falls. His father Paul disagreed, observing that it was wrong to charge money for viewing God's handiwork and that the Hulls had lost the respect of the city by doing so.

Curt persevered, eventually constructing a ticket booth adjoining the east boundary of Mushroom Park and occasionally erecting fences around Balanced Rock. He advertised, "Admission price of 50 cents includes the observatory, Indian show and Kodak privileges."

In 1909, the City of Colorado Springs established Garden of the Gods, the free public park created with the gift of land from the Perkins family. Mushroom Park not only adjoined the new Colorado Springs park on the west side but also abutted the city limits of Manitou on its south side.

Manitou officials could not have been pleased that the only entrance to the new park from their city was through the privately owned Mushroom Park, which charged admission. So, in 1909, Manitou inaugurated a legal challenge for ownership of Balanced Rock. Lawsuits focused on whether the road between Balanced Rock and Steamboat Rock was private or public. Manitou guidebooks claimed, "The Balanced Rock and Mushroom Park are private property, and an admission charge is made to the fenced-off portion, although no charge is made to drive over the public road."

Paul Goerke & Son now had three locations: Balanced Rock, Gateway Garden of the Gods, and an office at 241 Manitou Avenue. Their curio shop behind Steamboat Rock had been expanded to include a successful lunch counter.

Soon after their marriage in Germany, Paul and Ida Goerke immigrated to the United States in 1876. Their two sons, Curt and Benno, were both born in Colorado. The Goerke family had settled in Manitou Springs by 1887, the same year their younger son, Benno, died from a fall off the roof of a Manitou building. (Colorado Springs Pioneers Museum.)

Buena Vista Drive was the name of the road between Balanced Rock and Steamboat Rock when William Henry Jackson took this photograph about 1890. These rocks would become the featured attractions of Paul Goerke's Mushroom Park, which he developed after taking possession of the land. (William Henry Jackson Collection [Scan No. 20100198], History Colorado.)

In 1892, Paul Goerke contracted to purchase about 40 acres of land that included unusual rock formations resembling toadstools, in addition to Balanced Rock and Steamboat Rock. On July 22, 1898, Goerke opened Mushroom Park, an attraction developed upon his land, and proclaimed it a "delightful resort for lovers of sylvan retreats."

Mushroom Park was only a short walk of a half mile from the Manitou streetcar line. The Goerkes lined the road to the park with benches and picnic spots. They built a pavilion on Manitou Avenue for the use of visitors to the park to await the next trolley once they had completed their tour.

Keystone View Company published a stereoview in 1898 of Curt Goerke photographing tourists at Balanced Rock. Shortly after his father obtained Mushroom Park, Curt learned to take photographs from a man who had a picture stand set up by the attraction. Eventually, Curt made enough money to buy out the photographer.

The Goerkes built a curio store and lemonade stand in the shadow of Steamboat Rock that was later enlarged into a photography studio. The building was demolished in the 1930s. Curt Goerke carved steps to the top of Steamboat Rock and installed iron railings and telescopes that allowed views of Garden of the Gods park and surroundings.

The edge of the Goerke photography studio can be seen behind Steamboat Rock about 1900. Tourists on the observatory at the top of Steamboat had a panoramic view of Mushroom Park. The sign on the railings stated, "Steamboat Rock Observatory. Use of the Telescopes Free to the Visitors—All Welcome."

Curt Goerke stands at the base of Balanced Rock about 1905. Within a few years, Balanced Rock had become one of the most famous attractions in the Pikes Peak region, advertised as the "8th Wonder of the World." Goerke proclaimed it "the most photographed object in the U.S." By 1910, Goerke began to charge 50¢ admission to Mushroom Park.

Paul Goerke & Son specialized in souvenir photographs of tourists posing in front of Balanced Rock, often astride burros that the Goerkes provided. The first offerings were cabinet cards consisting of large photographs mounted on cardboard backings. Duplicate photographs could be ordered, at 25¢ each; orders were placed using the number on the front of the picture.

In 1903, a Folding Pocket Kodak camera was introduced that produced postcard-sized images. This invention generated the ensuing popularity of real-photo postcards. Goerke quickly adopted the more popular postcard format. For this real-photo postcard, two tourists pose on mules in the road leading to Balanced Rock. Duplicates of these postcards were only 10¢ each.

Charles Strausenback worked at least one summer at Balanced Rock taking photographs of tourists. He is seen here at far right behind the camera at the base of Steamboat Rock. He may have been employed by Curt Goerke as manager of the Balanced Rock curio shop and studio. (Garden of the Gods Trading Post.)

Pueblo Indians from New Mexico were hired to add native color by performing dances and posing for photographs. One of the first hired was Antonio Silva from Santa Clara Pueblo. Here, he stands at right with his hand on a tourist's shoulder. The group is in front of Goerke's ticket office for Mushroom Park. The little girl second from left is Agapita Silva, daughter of Antonio.

Photographs were not the only keepsakes available for tourists to purchase at Balanced Rock. Among other souvenirs sold in the Goerkes' curio store at the turn of the 20th century was this cast-metal inkwell in the shape of Balanced Rock.

By 1902, Paul Goerke & Son also had a location at 241 Manitou Avenue. Photographs were taken here at the start of mule trips to the top of Pikes Peak via the Manitou Burro Lines. When the tourists returned to Manitou, the photographs were developed and ready for purchase.

In 1900, Eastman Kodak Company introduced the Brownie camera, and photography became a hobby that nearly everyone could afford. These photographs of Balanced Rock are examples of turn-of-the-century snapshots taken with a personal camera. The photographer wrote on the image at left, "The great Balancing Rock, took this picture myself." The accessibility of portable cameras had a negative impact on the Goerkes' photography business; their revenue decreased greatly. Soon after, they began to charge admission to view Balanced Rock. At one point in 1904, Curt Goerke even tried to capitalize on the new technology and advertised camera rentals for 25¢ per day, also offering next-day service for film development.

*Four*

# ROCKS OF CONTENTION

In 1909, after Garden of the Gods was established as a free public park, Manitou officials were unhappy that the only entrance from their city into the popular new park was through the privately owned Mushroom Park. Consequently, Manitou challenged the Goerke family for ownership of the property, particularly for the road running through it. Every maneuver and strategy taken by the Goerkes and the Town of Manitou during the legal battle for Balanced Rock was substantially covered by the *Colorado Springs Gazette*, beginning with the article "Balanced Rock Is Bone of Contention," published on April 7, 1909:

> Whether or not Paul Goerke and his son, Curt, Manitou photographers, have the sole right to take photographs of their property, the famous Balanced Rock, in the Garden of the Gods, from the road running by the rock will probably soon be tested in the courts. No question as to the ownership of the Balanced Rock by the Goerkes is raised but numerous tourists trying to take photographs of the rock have gotten into trouble with the photographic firm, which claims ownership of the road passing the famous scenic attraction. According to the county commissioners, the thoroughfare, formerly a county road, was recently annexed by Manitou, and that town, whose ownership the Goerkes contest, will probably be made defendant in a test case to be instituted by the photographers. Photographs of the Balanced Rock, in common with those of other points of interest in the Garden of the Gods, are sold by the thousands every summer, and are carried away to all parts of the country, so that the commercial value of the monopoly claimed by the Goerkes is apparent.

Once the Goerkes erected a fence across the disputed road, the Town of Manitou filed a lawsuit in March 1910 claiming the wrongful withholding of property and arguing for the recovery of "the east two-thirds of the Balanced Rock and the west one-half of Steamboat Rock." Manitou claimed when the town was incorporated the roadway between the rocks was included within its limits, and thereby became a public street.

A jury decided in favor of Manitou in January 1911; the Goerkes announced they would appeal, and if defeated again, they would carry the case to the US Supreme Court. As the legal battles ensued, Paul Goerke died on May 30, 1913, and was buried in the Crystal Valley Cemetery.

A court of appeals reversed the earlier decision and awarded all rights to the Goerkes in January 1914. Shortly thereafter, Curt Goerke erected a 10-foot-high board fence around Balanced Rock and charged admission to see the attraction. This continued to aggravate Manitou officials.

In 1920, Goerke laid claim to the eastern boundary of his property abutting Garden of the Gods by installing a ticket booth to Mushroom Park at the intersection of Garden Lane and Beckers Lane. Charles Strausenback operated the ticket booth along with his Garden of the Gods Curio Company from a wood building to the east of the ticket booth.

When the estate of Jacob Becker, an original homesteader of land near the Garden of the Gods, came up for auction in 1921, Goerke imagined he had found a way to end the legal battle with Manitou. He purchased the 120-acre Becker Tract that included Beckers Lane, a road leading into the park from Manitou that did not pass through Goerke's property. In August 1922, he offered to deed Beckers Lane to Manitou, and in exchange pledged to remove the fence provided that the town agreed to give up all claims to and vacate the road at Balanced Rock. Town officials rejected Goerke's offer, and the battles began again with renewed vigor and intensity. Soon after, Goerke was arrested and jailed because "Manitou officials received word that the free public road had been obstructed with a fence, which had nailed to it a sign reading 'Alleged public road closed.' Puzzled automobilists were made to pass over another road and pay toll charges for the privilege of doing so."

When Manitou refused to accept Beckers Lane, Curt Goerke built a Pueblo-themed curio store abutting the existing entrance gate and ticket office to Mushroom Park, which had been renamed West Garden of the Gods. The new store, called the Indian, on the south slope of Grand View Hill, and the ticket office were operated by Charles Strausenback. Goerke continued to run the operations at Balanced Rock, charged admission for entrance to the property from the south, and struggled over the ownership of the road leading from Manitou.

In January 1930, a decision by a court of appeals affirmed lower-court decisions that Curt Goerke could not block the disputed road in order to charge admission to view Balanced Rock. Acting on a threat made nearly 20 years earlier, Goerke instructed his lawyer to petition the US Supreme Court for relief from the appeals court decision. In May 1931, the Supreme Court decided in favor of the Town of Manitou.

Curt Paul Goerke was born in Canon City, Colorado, on March 23, 1877. This portrait was likely taken in 1897, his senior year of high school. After graduation, he attended Colorado College. He was described as tall, medium build, with blue eyes and dark brown hair. After the decades-long fight with Manitou over ownership of Balanced Rock, he sold his property to Colorado Springs in 1932. Along with his wife and daughter, he then moved to Long Beach, California. There, he worked as a real estate broker until about 1937, when he opened Goerke's Social Security Club offering accounting services. Curt Goerke passed away in Los Angeles on March 7, 1958; his daughter Grace Boughner brought his remains back to Manitou to be buried next to his brother and parents in Crystal Valley Cemetery. (Colorado Springs Pioneers Museum.)

In March 1910, the Town of Manitou launched a legal challenge for the recovery of "the east two-thirds of the Balanced Rock and the west one-half of Steamboat Rock," claiming the narrow road between the rocks, which they had annexed the previous year, was a public street incorporated into the town limits. The Goerkes maintained the road was part of their property.

Even though the Goerkes fenced their property, tourists continued to enter without paying an admission fee. Leroy and Earl sit between the toadstools in Mushroom Park about 1920, apparently having hopped the barbed-wire fence in the foreground to attain their perch among the rocks.

The first court case against the Goerkes was decided in favor of Manitou in 1911. Curt Goerke then erected a high board fence around Balanced Rock and charged admission to enter. His efforts to fence off Balanced Rock from public view were thwarted endlessly by Manitou, which tore down the fences nearly as quickly as Goerke erected them.

In 1920, Charles Strausenback partnered with Curt Goerke in a curio shop and ticket booth on the eastern boundary of Mushroom Park. Strausenback, then 30 years old, had operated various curio businesses in and around Garden of the Gods for the previous two decades. (Garden of the Gods Trading Post.)

Charles Strausenback made this lithograph of Balanced Rock in the 1930s, but he had been producing easel art as early as 1914. A self-taught artist, he frequently copied his subjects from photographs and postcards, as was the case with this view of Balanced Rock.

Curt Goerke laid claim to the eastern boundary of Mushroom Park abutting Garden of the Gods by installing a ticket booth at the intersection of Garden Lane and Beckers Lane (where the Trading Post now stands). Charles Strausenback operated his Garden of the Gods Curio Company from this wood building adjacent to the ticket booth. Summertime was busy with tourists, as the 1920 photograph below indicates. (Below, Garden of the Gods Trading Post.)

Indian making Silver Jewelry

One of the main attractions for visitors to Charles Strausenback's curio businesses was the demonstration of silversmithing by Pueblo or Navajo artists. Epifanio Tafoya, from Santa Clara Pueblo, was the first silversmith to work for Strausenback. In this 1920 photograph, tourists look on from the door as Tafoya hammers silver on a tree stump on the porch of Garden of the Gods Curio Company, adjacent to the ticket office for Balanced Rock. Epifanio worked seasonally in the Pikes Peak area in the 1920s, and worked silver at Manitou Cliff Dwellings in 1924 but returned to working for Strausenback at the Indian around 1925. (Kelly Kilgore Chilcott Collection, Billie Jane Baguley Library and Archives, Heard Museum, Phoenix, Arizona, RC366[1]:20.)

A Pueblo Indian employee of Charles Strausenback, photographed on August 29, 1920, stands outside Garden of the Gods Curio Company. In the background is the ticket booth for Mushroom Park and Balanced Rock; at the time, Goerke was embroiled in lawsuits with Manitou because he charged admission to Mushroom Park.

Strausenback's Indian employees frequently brought the whole family to Garden of the Gods to work during the summer months. In 1920, Antonio Silva from Santa Clara Pueblo is accompanied by his daughter, Agapita Silva, second from left, and what are presumed to be other relatives.

Goerke and Strausenback frequently photographed their Indian employees in Garden of the Gods and printed the pictures as souvenir postcards. Here, Antonio Silva from Santa Clara Pueblo poses near Balanced Rock for a real-photo postcard made by Paul Goerke & Son. The postcards were given to the Indians to sell to tourists.

Agapita Silva, from Santa Clara Pueblo, dances near Balanced Rock. Curt Goerke's fence can be seen in the background. When Charles Strausenback partnered with Goerke in 1920, he also took over some of Goerke's curio stock. The back of this postcard is printed "Paul Goerke & Son," but stamped over in ink with "Garden of the Gods Curio Co, E. Strausenback Proprietor."

Curt Goerke purchased the 120-acre Becker Tract in 1921 for $3,000 and erected an entrance gate and ticket booth to Mushroom Park at the bottom of Grand View Hill. Goerke thought he had found a way to end the legal battle with Manitou when he purchased the tract, as it included a road leading into Garden of the Gods from Manitou that did not pass through Mushroom Park. Goerke hoped to deed the road, called Beckers Lane, to Manitou, and in exchange, he pledged to remove the fence around Balanced Rock provided that the town agreed to give up all claims to the road at the famous rock. Ultimately, Manitou rejected Goerke's offer, and the legal battles began again. (Both, Kelly Kilgore Chilcott Collection, Billie Jane Baguley Library and Archives, Heard Museum, Phoenix, Arizona; above, RC366[1]:78; below, RC366[1]:79.)

Once Manitou refused to accept the road through the Becker Tract, Curt Goerke built a Pueblo-themed curio store in 1924 that abutted the entrance gate and ticket office to Mushroom Park on the south slope of Grand View Hill. The new store, called the Indian, was operated by Charles Strausenback, who noted on the back of this photograph, "The new Place but the same old Hudson." Some of Strausenback's Indian employees stand out front, including silversmith Epifanio Tafoya, Santa Clara Pueblo. Curt Goerke advertised in the *Colorado Springs Gazette Telegraph* in 1924 that visitors to Balanced Rock on Sundays would be entertained by "the story of the fourteen-year-old contest between the owner and the town of Manitou." (Kelly Kilgore Chilcott Collection, Billie Jane Baguley Library and Archives, Heard Museum, Phoenix, Arizona, RC366[1]:31.2.)

These men took advantage of the "Kodak privileges" that came with paid admission to Mushroom Park, allowing access through the fence to take personal photographs of Balanced Rock. Curt Goerke was arrested in Manitou multiple times for "obstruction of a public road by a fence." Once, in 1922, after Manitou officials tore down the boards, Goerke was found erecting another barrier farther up the road; police arrested him and escorted him to jail.

In January 1930, an appeals court decided that Curt Goerke could not block the disputed road in order to charge admission to view Balanced Rock, since the road was considered a public highway. Goerke then petitioned the US Supreme Court for relief.

The Supreme Court decided in favor of the Town of Manitou in May 1931, giving the town the right-of-way to the road running through Curt Goerke's property. After decades of wrangling with Manitou, Goerke had accumulated much debt, and he finally decided to divest himself of the property. His 275 acres were sold to the City of Colorado Springs in February 1932 for a mere $25,000. Manitou relinquished all rights and right-of-way to the property, allowing it to be incorporated into the Garden of the Gods public city park. Local newspapers announced that ceremonies would be held February 20, 1932, for the "Emancipation of Balanced Rock," and dignitaries from Colorado Springs and Manitou would oversee the tearing down of the high board fence. All residents of the region were invited to attend, and a large crowd participated. (Photograph by Stewarts Commercial Photographers, © Pikes Peak Library District, 013-10181.)

# Five

# ENTRANCE TO THE WEST

In 1924, Curt Goerke consolidated two separate parcels of his land, Mushroom Park and the Becker Tract, and renamed the new parcel West Garden of the Gods. Goerke's property contained Grand View Hill, which not only provided magnificent views of Pikes Peak but also shared a half-mile frontage with the free public park Garden of the Gods. The expansion of his tourist attraction provided an entrance adjacent to the park; at this entrance, Goerke planned to erect a grand Pueblo Indian–style structure next to the ticket booth and archway. The Indian was built on the south slope of Grand View Hill, which is now the parking lot for the Spring Canyon South Picnic Area.

Goerke committed $30,000 for the construction of the Indian. A full-page article in the *Colorado Springs Sunday Gazette and Telegraph—Annual Edition* on March 2, 1924, detailed the construction plans. Goerke hired a renowned Santa Fe architect to design a faithful reproduction of an Indian pueblo that would serve as a curio store, museum, and ticket office for the West Garden of the Gods.

Goerke's initial plans were to build a four-story terraced structure: on one story, Pueblo Indians would perform dances, on another would be a refreshment stand, and other terraces would be used as observatories. Rocks found on the nearby cliffs would be used in the construction. However, when the Indian opened for the 1924 summer season, it only comprised a single story with a decorative cupola on one corner, while Charles Strausenback's hand-painted reproductions of Navajo sand paintings on the interior walls conveyed the Southwestern theme inside the building.

Charles and Esther Strausenback moved their business, Garden of the Gods Curio Company, into the new building and made it their residence from 1924 to 1929. Charles was ideally suited to run the new store; not only had he been engaged in the curio business in the Garden of the Gods since 1900, but according to the *Gazette*, he "has had many years experience with the Indians and as salesman of souvenirs. As a lad he was employed by Fred Harvey to sell Indian blankets on the Santa Fe trains from Los Angeles to Albuquerque."

Before the opening of the Indian in 1924, Charles Strausenback traveled to New Mexico and Arizona to secure the Pueblo and Navajo employees who would work there. These employees constructed Navajo-style hogans on the grounds, built from logs gathered in the nearby forest. These served as residences for the craftspeople and their families during the summer months.

The stated purpose of bringing Native Americans to the Garden of the Gods was so tourists could have the opportunity to see the Indians "plying their native crafts, each an expert in his chosen occupation." The finished goods would be available for display and sale in the showroom.

It was at the Indian that Strausenback made his first mark as an Indian trader. The jewelry that was designed and made there between 1924 and 1929 was unique, with stamped figural designs including thunderbirds, whirling logs, arrows, and squash blossoms on hand-hammered ingot coin silver. Strausenback hired Navajo silversmith William Goodluck, who was joined by Santa Clara Pueblo silversmith Epifanio Tafoya and his nephew Severo Tafoya, who learned to work silver at the shop.

The Indian was advertised as "the only trading post in Colorado where you can see the Navajos and Pueblo Indians, making silver jewelry, weaving blankets and working at their native arts. This is undoubtedly the largest and finest reproduction of an Indian pueblo in the Pikes Peak region." And Strausenback made it a success, as it was estimated that in the summers, 1,500 to 1,800 visitors a day passed through the store. On one occasion, 3,000 people were entertained.

Nevertheless, as Goerke's legal battle continued with the Town of Manitou, Charles Strausenback was making plans for his future. In the summer of 1926, he applied for copyright of a new logo for his business; his design depicted a Pueblo or Tewa thunderbird figure pouncing on a rattlesnake. Once the copyright was granted on July 24, Strausenback changed the name of the business to "Garden of the Gods Trading Company," which still operated out of the Indian.

Also in 1926, Charles and Esther purchased 20 acres of land from Anna Becker, widow of the original homesteader Jacob Becker. It was the same land where the Strausenbacks had operated Garden of the Gods Curio Company from a wood building in 1920. The parcel was only a short distance from the Indian, a little over a tenth of a mile, at the intersection of Beckers Lane and Garden Lane. For the next three years, the Strausenbacks continued to run the Indian while they prepared to erect a trading post on their own land.

In 1929, construction on the Trading Post on Beckers Lane was completed, and the Strausenbacks moved their business permanently to their own building. After Strausenback vacated the Indian, it was not occupied by another concession, and the building on Grand View Hill was likely torn down in 1932.

This painting of the Indian was created by Charles Strausenback in 1924, copied from the architectural drawing by T. Charles Gaastra, an architect hired by Curt Goerke to design the building. It was to be a faithful representation of an Indian pueblo and serve as a curio store, museum, and ticket office for the West Garden of the Gods; Goerke committed $30,000 for its construction. The initial plans were impressive; it was to be a multistoried, terraced structure, with the main floor housing a museum and a large showroom for selling Indian curios and relics, while smaller rooms were to be occupied by Navajo and Pueblo Indians demonstrating their crafts. The construction would use rocks found on the nearby cliffs and would be covered with cement to represent the Indian adobe construction. The store would be managed by Charles Strausenback. (Garden of the Gods Trading Post.)

SEE THE PETRIFIED INDIAN (CLIFF DWELLER) FREE
AT "THE INDIAN"

# GARDEN OF THE GODS CURIO CO.

GARDEN OF THE GODS, COLORADO

Hyland 106-J
CHAS. E. STRAUSENBACK

P. O. BOX 686
COLORADO SPRINGS

Charles Strausenback printed his first business cards about 1924 while operating his Garden of the Gods Curio Company out of the Indian trading post. Printed on the reverse is a list of stereotypical Indian-style designs with romantic interpretations, such as "Thunderbird = Prosperity, Good Fortune and Happiness are unlimited."

Upon completion in 1924, the Indian fell shy of the initial grand plans; it was only a single story with a decorative cupola on one corner. The exterior was left in a rough state and not finished smooth as designed. The sign over the entrance gate reads, "West Garden of the Gods," after Goerke consolidated the Becker Tract with Mushroom Park and renamed the attraction.

Above, the Indian trading post was photographed for souvenir pictures in 1924 with three Santa Clara Pueblo Indians standing in front. From left to right are O-Yegy-On't-Ya, Don Ying'ye, and his spouse Pobe Senge. An unidentified Indian man, wrapped in a striped blanket, stands on the roof. The entrance gate to West Garden of the Gods is to the right, or north, of the building. The Manitou Incline can be seen as a white line running from the chimney up Mount Manitou. Situated on Grand View Hill, which Curt Goerke purchased in 1921, the land is now part of Garden of the Gods park and is the parking lot for the Spring Canyon South Picnic Area. The building was likely demolished in 1932, when the City of Colorado Springs purchased the land and annexed it to the park. The site is seen below as it appears today.

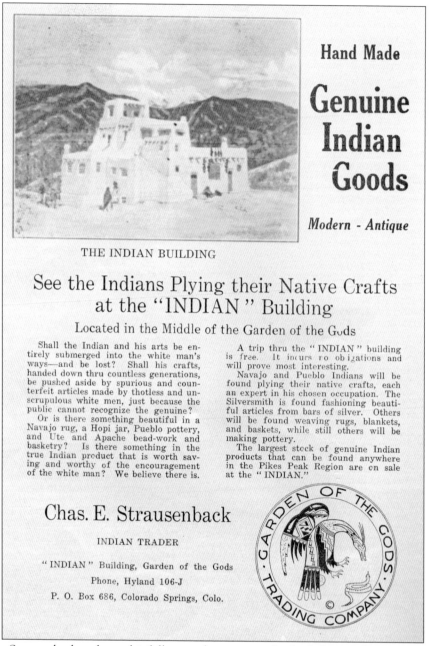

Charles Strausenback took out this full-page advertisement for the Indian in the *Manitou Springs Journal Annual Edition* of May 1928, where he boasted, "The largest stock of genuine Indian products that can be found anywhere in the Pikes Peak Region are on sale at the 'INDIAN.'" His inventory included modern and antique genuine Indian goods. In the same issue, Strausenback wrote a multipage article titled, "Native Indian Hand-Craft as Found in the Southwest," where he promoted the virtues of Southwest Indian crafts. During the winter months, Strausenback traveled to Arizona and New Mexico to hire silversmiths, weavers, and potters to demonstrate their crafts in the summers, "each an expert in his chosen occupation," as advertised. The artists not only worked their crafts, but also entertained the tourists with dances.

About 1926, while managing the Indian, Charles Strausenback printed new business cards to reflect the name change of his company to Garden of the Gods Trading Company after he copyrighted the Tewa Thunderbird logo. At this time, he began to identify himself as an "Indian trader" and not as a curio dealer.

SEE THE PETRIFIED INDIAN (CLIFF DWELLER)
FREE AT "THE INDIAN"

GARDEN OF THE GODS, COLORADO

GARDEN OF THE GODS · TRADING COMPANY

GENUINE INDIAN GOODS

CHAS. E. STRAUSENBACK
INDIAN TRADER

HYLAND ████ 48          P. O. BOX 686
COLORADO SPRINGS, COLO.

The Indian with ticket office and entry arch to Goerke's West Garden of the Gods on the right, seen here about 1925, was situated on the south slope of Grand View Hill, affording magnificent views of Pikes Peak. On the far right can be seen the Pueblo kiva and Navajo hogan built by the Indian families who lived there. (Garden of the Gods Trading Post.)

Charles Strausenback is pictured around 1925 at the Indian wearing beaded, Plains-style moccasins and a silver bracelet on his wrist. At this time, he was making plans to build his own trading post. (Kelly Kilgore Chilcott Collection, Billie Jane Baguley Library and Archives, Heard Museum, Phoenix, Arizona, RC366[1]:42.)

About 1925, Esther Strausenback is seen holding two coyote pups in her arms outside of the Indian. Garden of the Gods can be seen in the background. (Kelly Kilgore Chilcott Collection, Billie Jane Baguley Library and Archives, Heard Museum, Phoenix, Arizona, RC366[1]:49.)

Charles Strausenback (left) stands in front of the Indian about 1925 with Santa Clara Pueblo Indian O-Yegy-On't-Ya ("Frost at Sunrise"), otherwise known as Juan Jose Gutierrez. Between them is an unfinished weaving by Gutierrez with the initials "CES." Strausenback noted on the back of the photograph, "A special blanket made for me this summer." (Kelly Kilgore Chilcott Collection, Billie Jane Baguley Library and Archives, Heard Museum, Phoenix, Arizona, RC366[1]:39.)

O-Yegy-Ont-Ya was Juan Jose Gutierrez from Santa Clara Pueblo. He was photographed for this souvenir postcard standing in front of the Indian. The front of the postcard states he was born in 1838, but his actual birth date was closer to 1856. The sender wrote on the back before mailing this postcard on July 2, 1924, that she "was talking to this Indian today."

Epifanio Tafoya (Na-Na-Ping) worked as a silversmith for Charles Strausenback from as early as 1920. He was born about 1879 in Santa Clara Pueblo and died in 1933. Epifanio probably taught silversmithing to his nephew Severo Tafoya (Ca-Ping), who accompanied his uncle to the Indian to work in the 1920s.

William Goodluck, identified on this souvenir postcard by his Navajo name, Host-Nat-Woty, stands near the Indian. This postcard was mailed on July 16, 1927. The sender wrote to Lelah May Hathaway, a former teacher at Carlisle Indian School, "We stopped this morning at the Garden of the Gods and there I met Wm Goodluck who was once your pupil. He is a silversmith (Navajo) . . . He gave me this picture to send you."

Beginning in the early 1920s, William Goodluck and his family traveled to the Pikes Peak region to work for Charles Strausenback during the summers. This photograph was taken inside the Indian, where Goodluck is shown working silver while his wife, Yekanasbah, weaves at her loom and their children spin and card the wool. Strausenback painted the mural of a Navajo sandpainting that can be seen in the background.

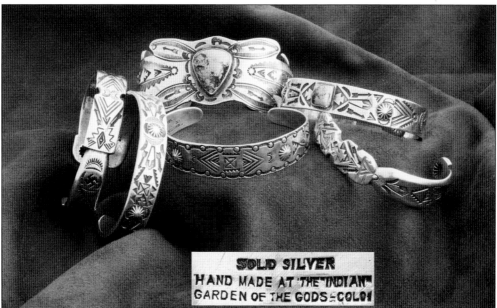

These six silver bracelets made about 1925 at the Indian are hallmarked, "Solid Silver Hand Made At The "Indian" Garden Of The Gods—Colo." They were made by the Pueblo and Navajo silversmiths working for Charles Strausenback. The top bracelet is similar in design to one that William Goodluck wears in the photograph on the opposite page, so it is very likely that he made this piece.

Santa Clara Pueblo Indian Severo Tafoya (Ca-Ping) stands in the doorway of the Navajo hogan near the Indian. The hogan was built in traditional Navajo fashion by the Indians using logs gathered from nearby, and no nails were used in its construction. It served as the residence for families who worked there in the summers.

Marie Porfilia Tafoya (Ja-Ro), Santa Clara Pueblo, lived with her husband, Severo, year-round at the Indian in the Navajo hogan. She is shown in traditional Pueblo attire working at an upright loom inside the Indian. It was not customary for Pueblo women to weave, and Ja-Ro used a nontraditional Spanish loom and carpet yarn to make her textiles.

Santa Clara Pueblo Indian Severiano Naranjo (Don Ying'ye) was photographed by a tourist with his trunk and dance shield in 1925 in front of the Navajo hogan at the Indian. Naranjo worked as an entertainer for Charles Strausenback for a few years in the mid-1920s, bringing his family with him each summer.

Santa Clara Pueblo Indian boy Wha-Be came with his father Severiano Naranjo (Don Ying'ye) and family to the Pikes Peak region in the mid-1920s. Wha-Be was photographed numerous times by Charles Strausenback in various poses wearing a small Plains-style feathered headdress. The photographs were used as advertising postcards sold through Garden of the Gods Curio Company.

Two teenaged boys from Santa Clara Pueblo, Ta-It-Zah (left) and Co-It-Zah (below), were photographed in front of the Indian by Charles Strausenback for souvenir postcards in 1924 or 1925. Handwritten on the back of the card below is "Jose, June 22, 1925." Neither of these boys have yet been identified with their Christian names, but they were likely related to either Severiano Naranjo or Juan Jose Gutierrez. The Indian performers in the Pikes Peak region were dominated by families from Santa Clara Pueblo; this summertime excursion away from the reservation served as an important source of income.

*Six*

# A Lifetime
# in the Garden

On April 7, 1929, the *Colorado Springs Gazette* reported on a new Indian curio store about to open in the Pikes Peak region. The article, "New Indian Store in Garden of Gods," stated that Charles and Esther Strausenback spent $10,000 on the "Trading Post." The building was erected during the winter months and was of "the typical Pueblo type" with cupolas, and the exterior resembled real adobe. The main storeroom would be approximately 40 feet by 60 feet, with living quarters for the owners on the second floor. The article described Charles as "one of the outstanding Indian traders of the west," having made his reputation at the Indian a few years earlier.

The Trading Post opened for business on June 9, 1929. The occasion was accompanied by another article in the *Colorado Springs Gazette*, "Indians Transplanted to Garden of Gods in Strausenback's New 'Trading Post,' " stating that Strausenback's dream of a quarter century was finally realized. After 28 years in the curio business, from selling souvenirs at the side of the carriage road as a youngster, to operating stores in all parts of the park, and lately, at the Indian store in the south part of the park, he had built up a "large clientele of customers from all parts of the world."

The story also touted the Indians who were relocated to the new store to work in silver and weave blankets. Many of the artists who worked for Strausenback at the Indian also worked and lived at the new Trading Post. The property included two Navajo-style hogans where "four adult Navajos, a Navajo baby in its carrier and a family of Santa Claras are living at the trading post in Indian fashion." The four adult Navajos included silversmith Hosteen Goodluck, his son William Goodluck, plus William's wife, Yekanasbah, who worked as a weaver. From Santa Clara were Severo Tafoya and his wife, Porfilia. The article described Hosteen Goodluck as "one of the old types of Indian silver workers, disdaining modern bench conveniences for the methods of his forefathers." At that time, "Old Hosteen" was one of the best-known Navajo silversmiths. He was born in the southern part of the Navajo reservation about 1865 and died on March 26, 1937. He demonstrated silver in 1901 at the Pan-American Exposition in Buffalo, New York, and again in 1904 at the Louisiana Purchase Exposition in St. Louis, Missouri. Goodluck had been employed by renowned Zuni trader C.G. Wallace in the 1920s and was recognized as one of the most expert Indian silversmiths in the Southwest. He may have only worked for Strausenback during the summer of 1929.

Much of the advertising verbiage that was used for the Indian continued to be used for the Trading Post, as an early postcard stated the new building was "the only trading post in Colorado where you can see the Navajo and Pueblo Indians making silver jewelry, weaving blankets and working at their native arts."

Strausenback continued his buying trips to the Indian reservations, where he acquired stock for his trading post and maintained relationships with his Indian friends, some of whom agreed to come work for him in Colorado Springs. In these travels, he likely became acquainted with the famous San Ildefonso Pueblo artist Awa Tsireh, who became associated with Strausenback shortly after the Trading Post opened and worked there as a painter and silversmith in the 1930s and 1940s.

Strausenback's skills as an artist were put to good use on his new building. Not only did he paint a large version of his company logo above the porch, he also painted murals representing four of the major Southwestern Indian tribes on the exterior walls. One mural depicted a Pueblo woman emerging from a kiva; the others are of a Navajo sandpainting, a Zuni Shalako, and a Hopi Sunface Kachina. These murals are signed "Tong Say Ontya 1929." The *Gazette* article from April 7, 1929, stated that Charles and Esther "have been taken into the Tewa tribe of Indians as full-fledged members;" as such, they would have received Tewa names. The tribe was most likely Santa Clara Pueblo, as Charles had strong bonds with many of its members, and his Tewa name most likely was Tong Say Ontya.

Since the opening of the Indian, Strausenback identified himself as an Indian trader, and his business cards and building signage proclaimed him as such. To that effect, in 1934, he joined the United Indian Traders Association, a Gallup, New Mexico–based organization whose goals were the promotion and perpetuation of genuine hand-made Indian arts. Strausenback was a proud member, attending organization dinners in Phoenix, and even acknowledged his membership on business checks drawn on the Bank of Manitou.

During the winters of 1934 and 1935, the Strausenbacks lived in Miami, Florida, but Phoenix became their winter haunt from 1936 to 1948. Charles and Esther ran the Hotel Adams Gift Shop, which they renamed Strausenback's Indian Silver Shops in 1940.

Charles Strausenback made a painting of his new Pueblo-themed building that was used on postcards advertising "Strausenback's Trading Post," published in 1929. Strausenback took artistic license and situated the Trading Post on Grand View Hill. On the left side of the Trading Post in this painting, a Navajo hogan and a Pueblo-style kiva that were built by the Indian employees are depicted. In the foreground is the boundary fence for Garden of the Gods park.

The above design of a Tewa Indian Thunderbird attacking a rattlesnake was painted by Charles Strausenback, adapted from paintings by Awa Tsireh. The painting was sent to the US Copyright Office, where it was received on July 24, 1926. The copyright was granted for the logo of Strausenback's business Garden of the Gods Trading Company. Strausenback painted this design on the façade of the Trading Post immediately after construction. (Both, Garden of the Gods Trading Post.)

Chas. E. Stranunbach,
Colorado Springs, Colo.
Indian Thunderbird. Design within a circle of the Indian thunder bird attacking a rattlesnake. Lettering around border.
By Chas. E. Stranunbach, of the United States.
Copy received July 24, 1926. Entry: Class G, XXc., No. 78266

[SEAL]

Thorvald Solberg
Register of Copyrights.

GOVERNMENT PRINTING OFFICE

This photograph, taken in 1929, was sold by Charles Strausenback as a souvenir of the Trading Post. Navajo silversmith William Goodluck and his family are pictured walking in front of the fence marking the boundary of the property with Garden of the Gods park. Beckers Lane is the dirt road at right.

On the porch of the Trading Post in the summer of 1929 are Strausenback's Indian employees. Porfilia and Severo Tafoya are at far left, renowned Navajo silversmith Hosteen Goodluck sits on the porch, his son William Goodluck hammers silver at a stump, and his wife and children sit nearby.

After the Trading Post opened in 1929, four murals were painted on the exterior walls of the porch and signed by Tong Say Ontya, which is believed to be the Tewa name given to Charles Strausenback. The *Colorado Springs Gazette* reported that Charles and Esther had been taken into the Tewa tribe, likely at Santa Clara Pueblo, where Charles had strong bonds with many members. The Pueblo woman emerging from a kiva above is patterned after a painting by Awa Tsireh. At left is a Zuni Shalako copied from an illustration by M. Wright Gill made in 1900. (Both, Garden of the Gods Trading Post.)

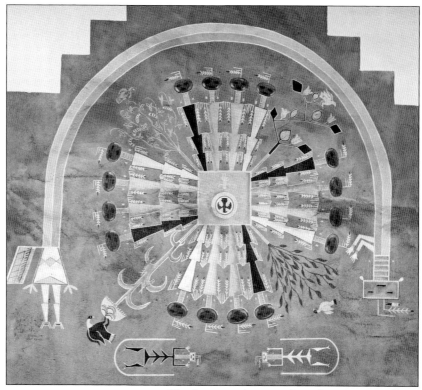

The four murals painted on the exterior walls of the porch of the Trading Post by Charles Strausenback represent four Southwestern tribes. The above mural depicts a Navajo sandpainting of sacred plants with Yei figures and an overarching rainbow god. At left is a Hopi Sunface Kachina. These 90-year-old murals remain vibrant, having been professionally restored through the years. (Both, Garden of the Gods Trading Post.)

The opaque watercolor painting of a Pueblo corn dance above is signed "Tong Say Ontya 1933," and also in pencil, "Strausenback 1933," indicating that Charles Strausenback painted under both names. Below is a lithograph entitled *Corn Dance* made by Strausenback in 1939, which is nearly identical except for added background. The lithograph is similar enough to the original painting to indicate that Strausenback was the artist of both. (Above, private collection.)

This early 1930s photograph of the Trading Post hangs in its art gallery. The Strausenbacks spent $10,000 to construct the building in the style of Pueblo Indian dwellings, with vigas for roof supports, cupolas, and the exterior resembling real adobe. It was erected during the winter of 1928–1929. The main sales area measured approximately 40 feet by 60 feet, and the owners resided in small quarters on the second floor above the store. Beckers Lane runs to the west of the building, and the park boundary is marked by both a fence and parking bumpers. (Garden of the Gods Trading Post.)

The adobe fireplace in the main sales area of the Trading Post was designed and painted by Charles Strausenback during construction in 1929 and still stands in original condition. Clay tiles with Pueblo designs were inlaid into the surface, and Strausenback painted Navajo Yeis and a Pueblo-cloud design on the front. (Garden of the Gods Trading Post.)

In the early 1930s, husband and wife Severo and Porfilia Tafoya stand in front of their residence, a separate Pueblo-style building constructed just behind the Trading Post. The Tafoyas were the only Indians working for Strausenback who made Colorado Springs their permanent, year-round residence.

In the late 1920s, Charles Strausenback constructed an archway over Garden Lane, just north of Grand View Hill where the road intersects with Garden Drive. The above sign reads, "To Balanced Rock & Manitou Spgs Via Strausenback Trading Post 3/10 Mi., See The Indians," and directed tourists to the Indian. In the 1930s, Strausenback replaced the sign on the roadway arch (below) directing tourists to his trading post. About 1940, the sign read, "Balanced Rock and Manitou Springs, Direct Route Via The Trading Post." (Below, Kelly Kilgore Chilcott Collection, Billie Jane Baguley Library and Archives, Heard Museum, Phoenix, Arizona, RC366[1]:77.)

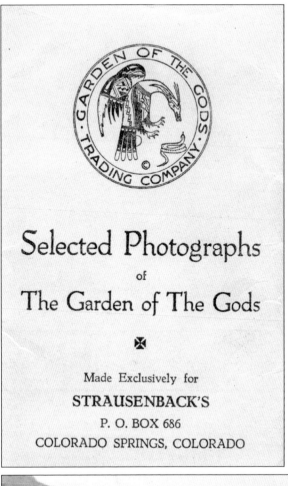

# Selected Photographs

of

# The Garden of The Gods

✠

Made Exclusively for

**STRAUSENBACK'S**

P. O. BOX 686

COLORADO SPRINGS, COLORADO

Keepsake photographs of scenic attractions were popular tourist souvenirs during the first half of the 20th century. Charles Strausenback routinely sold packets of "Selected Photographs" of Garden of the Gods, many of them branded with his logo and mailing address. The packets contained images of rock formations in the park. Included in the souvenir packets was the below photograph of the Trading Post taken in the 1930s. Only during this period did the sign on the building state, "Free See the Indian Silversmiths;" the Trading Post had gained recognition for its production of silver jewelry by this time.

The Strausenbacks were not content to operate the Trading Post as their only business venture. They also ran various other Indian curio stores in the Pikes Peak region. In 1930, they managed the curio shop at Cheyenne Lodge, a rustic Pueblo-themed resort owned by the Broadmoor Hotel at the top of Cheyenne Mountain. Strausenback sometimes brought Navajo silversmith William Goodluck and his family to work at the lodge. Goodluck would demonstrate the techniques of silversmithing while his wife wove Navajo rugs.

In 1930, the Strausenbacks operated the curio concession at the Ute Chief Spring Pavilion between Manitou Avenue and Fountain Creek. As seen above in September 1929, the building appears to have been newly constructed. The statue of an Indian pouring mineral water from a jug was originally made of plaster. As with all of the curio businesses managed by the Strausenbacks, a Pueblo Indian (left) identified only as Seva Klanis, entertained the tourists at the pavilion. The building still stands but has been abandoned for years.

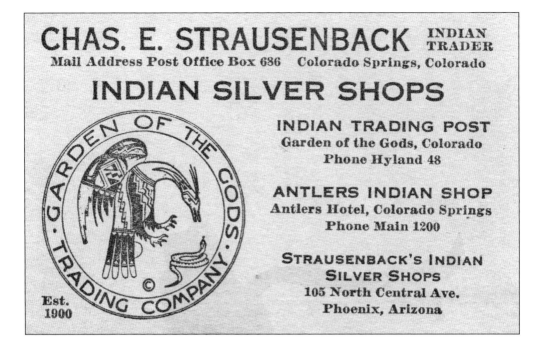

# CHAS. E. STRAUSENBACK INDIAN TRADER

Mail Address Post Office Box 636 Colorado Springs, Colorado

## INDIAN SILVER SHOPS

### INDIAN TRADING POST
Garden of the Gods, Colorado
Phone Hyland 48

### ANTLERS INDIAN SHOP
Antlers Hotel, Colorado Springs
Phone Main 1200

### STRAUSENBACK'S INDIAN SILVER SHOPS
105 North Central Ave.
Phoenix, Arizona

Est. 1900

GARDEN OF THE GODS · TRADING COMPANY ·

Charles Strausenback's business card about 1940 (above) stated that his business was established in 1900, when he would have been 10 years old and selling gypsum carvings in the park. The card also advertised his three main business ventures: the Trading Post, the Antlers Indian Shop, and Strausenback's Indian Silver Shops in the Adams Hotel in downtown Phoenix. From 1932 to 1945, the Strausenbacks managed the newsstand and Indian Shop at the Antlers Hotel (below) in downtown Colorado Springs. They had showcases of Indian jewelry by the elevators and a large room just off the lobby with Indian jewelry, rugs, and pottery for sale.

The Pueblo Indians employed by Charles Strausenback embarked on building an authentic kiva, or underground ceremonial chamber, at the northeast side of the Trading Post in the early 1930s. The finished structure was typical of the Tewa kivas found at villages in New Mexico. Above, Porfilia Tafoya exits the finished kiva while her husband, Severo Tafoya, approaches the stairs. Awa Tsireh beats a drum in the foreground. Below, Severo (Ca-Ping) and Porfilia (Ja-Ro) were photographed in front of the kiva in the late 1930s. (Above, Kelly Kilgore Chilcott Collection, Billie Jane Baguley Library and Archives, Heard Museum, Phoenix, Arizona, RC366[1]:69.)

Norman "Red" Hughes (left) owned the Red Cloud Inn in Cascade in the 1930s and 1940s. One of his stops on a promotional tour was at the Trading Post, where Charles Strausenback stood next to the ox-drawn covered wagon that announced, "Four Miles Up Ute Pass, On the Trail of the '49, to Red Cloud Inn, Mountain Trout, Dinners-Lunches." (Garden of the Gods Trading Post.)

It is unknown how the rationing and travel restrictions enacted during World War II affected the Strausenbacks' business. But after the war, in 1946, Abraham Bill Berner was hired to manage the Trading Post for a few years while Charles and Esther worked elsewhere. In the 1940s, the ubiquitous sign "Free See the Petrified Indian Inside" was painted on two sides of the building.

The only known photograph of Charles and Esther Strausenback together shows them standing on the porch of their Trading Post in the early 1940s. In the 1950s, they built a home on the hill south of the Trading Post and vacated the small living quarters on the second floor. Shortly after, Charles suffered a stroke and passed away on June 1, 1957, at the age of 66. He was cremated, and his ashes were scattered in the Garden of the Gods. Charles and Esther never had children, so Esther, who was Charles's business partner since their marriage, continued to run the Trading Post until her retirement. She passed away in Colorado Springs in 1995. (Kelly Kilgore Chilcott Collection, Billie Jane Baguley Library and Archives, Heard Museum, Phoenix, Arizona, RC366[1]:45.)

Charles Strausenback took this photograph of a group on the porch of the Trading Post in the early 1940s. The photograph was taken the same day as the one on the facing page. Standing from left to right are John Etsitty (Navajo silversmith who also went by the name Johnny Silversmith), unidentified (possibly John Etsitty's wife), unidentified, Esther Strausenback, unidentified boy (possibly John Etsitty's son), unidentified, and Severo and Porfilia Tafoya. (Kelly Kilgore Chilcott Collection, Billie Jane Baguley Library and Archives, Heard Museum, Phoenix, Arizona, RC366[1]:62.1.)

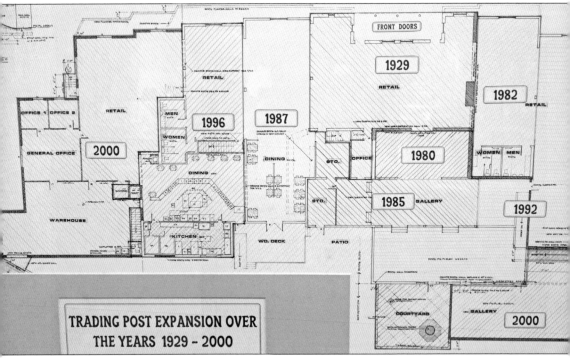

**TRADING POST EXPANSION OVER THE YEARS 1929 – 2000**

While maintaining Charles Strausenback's original concept, the Haas family has designed and built six expansions to Garden of the Gods Trading Post since they took possession of the property in 1979. On the northeast side, the Pueblo kiva was filled in, and the Navajo hogan dismantled in order to make room for an Indian art gallery. The original Trading Post encompassed 2,800 square feet. Now totaling 22,000 square feet under the leadership of Tim S. Haas, it is operated as a multi-featured business, including a gift shop, Indian art gallery, café, conference center, and wedding venue. Its largest sales are from Memorial Day to Labor Day, when it employs approximately 98 people; a reduced staff operates the business during the remainder of the year. (Garden of the Gods Trading Post.)

The exterior of Garden of the Gods Trading Post demonstrates the Haas family's commitment to maintaining the vision of Charles Strausenback. The wood portico, murals on the porch, and the building façade are intact from the original structure, conveying the ambiance of the Trading Post of nearly a century ago. Historic photographs of Strausenback, the Trading Post, and Garden of the Gods adorn the interior walls. The Indian art gallery is decorated with pieces of Strausenback's artwork, and antique display cases showcase Strausenback's miniature gypsum carvings, historic metalwork, and memorabilia. Wood frames on the walls display metalwork made by Awa Tsireh and other silversmiths who worked at the Trading Post.

Even though the Trading Post stayed open all year, business was likely slow in the winter months. The Strausenbacks spent the winters of 1936 to 1948 in Arizona, where they ran the Hotel Adams Gift Shop at 105 N. Central Avenue in downtown Phoenix. In 1940, they renamed the shop Strausenback's Indian Silver Shops. Hotel Adams was located in the heart of the lively Phoenix business district.

This sign hung above the entrance to Strausenback's Indian Silver Shops in Phoenix. In this shop, Strausenback employed Navajo and Pueblo silversmiths, some of whom worked in Phoenix in the winter and then at the Trading Post during the summer months. (Garden of the Gods Trading Post.)

The silversmithing tools, including workbenches and anvils on tree stumps, that were used at the Indian were moved to the Trading Post in 1929 and are now on display in the art gallery. In 1929, Strausenback had new hallmark stamps made plus a shop mark depicting the Tewa thunderbird logo. The stamping tools (above) are stored in their original wood boxes that were occasionally seen in historic photographs behind the silversmiths working at the anvils. (Both, Garden of the Gods Trading Post.)

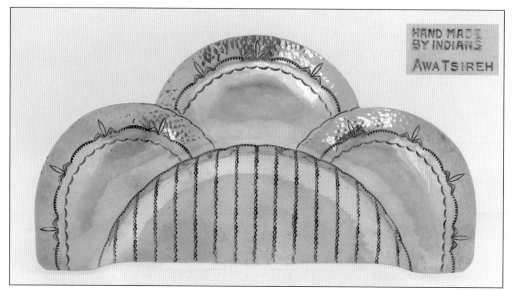

Shortly after the Trading Post opened, the famous Pueblo artist Awa Tsireh became associated with Strausenback and worked there as a painter and silversmith in the 1930s and 1940s. Awa Tsireh confirmed to anthropologist John Adair that he only made silver in the summers in Colorado Springs. Awa Tsireh worked not only with silver but also copper, nickel silver, and aluminum. He made the copper crumb tray above in the design of a Pueblo cloud, while the silver spoon, pin, pill box, and matchbook holder below were made in typical tourist style. He made the "V for Victory" pin at the beginning of World War II.

William Goodluck, his father, Hosteen Goodluck, and Severo Tafoya were the first silversmiths hired at the Trading Post. The metalwork made in the first few years included typical tourist-style design stamps like thunderbirds and crossed arrows. This copper tray was probably made by a Navajo silversmith, while the silver bird necklace was likely made by a Pueblo silversmith.

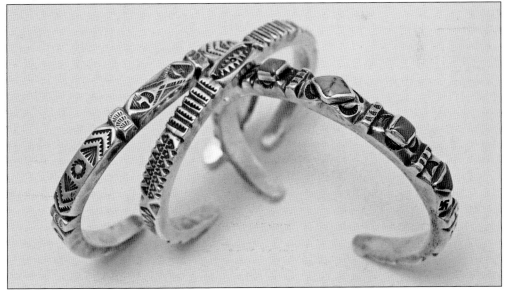

These three heavy silver ingot bracelets with stamp and file work were made at the Trading Post. The plain silver ones on the left were made by Awa Tsireh. The bracelet on the right with the turquoise settings was made in the style of Awa Tsireh by another of the silversmiths who worked there.

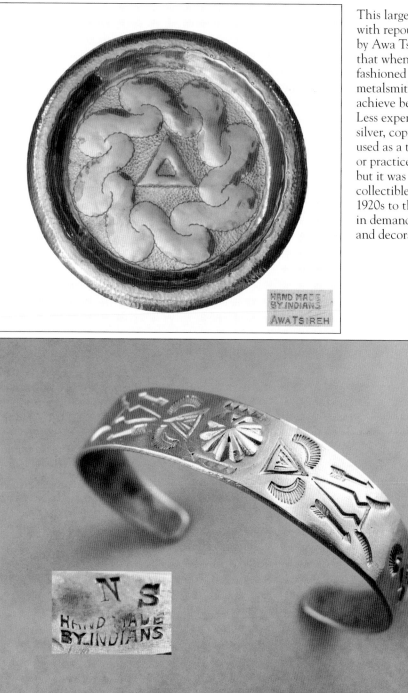

This large copper tray with repoussé work made by Awa Tsireh shows that when copper was fashioned by skilled metalsmiths, it could achieve beautiful results. Less expensive than silver, copper was often used as a teaching or practice material, but it was also highly collectible from the 1920s to the 1950s and in demand for wearable and decorative items.

This bracelet, made at the Trading Post in the 1930s, is hallmarked NS, indicating it was made from nickel silver. Among other silversmiths who worked for Strausenback were Awa Tsireh's younger brother Rafael "Ralph" Roybal and Charles Montoya. In the 1950s, Melvin Johnnie, Navajo, and Antonio Duran, from Picuris Pueblo, were probably the last silversmiths to work at the Trading Post.

Many silversmiths worked at the Trading Post over the years whose names have been lost to time. One as yet unidentified Navajo silversmith who worked for Strausenback used his personal hallmark of the initials BA with a Yei figure. He made this silver bracelet with agate settings in the 1930s; it includes the Trading Post shop marks.

Navajo silversmith David Taliman had a family connection to Colorado Springs. He married Anacita Naranjo from Santa Clara Pueblo, whose parents and brothers began working in the Pikes Peak region in the early 20th century. Taliman made this silver *ketoh*, or bow guard, style bracelet while working for Strausenback at the Trading Post.

Many articles of silver and copper were produced by the Indian silversmiths who worked for Strausenback, from wearable jewelry such as bracelets, rings, and pins to curios such as buttons, pill boxes, trays, tableware, and flatware. The design stamps on these pieces utilize uncomplicated elements combined in artistic ways to produce elegant effects.

This unique large sterling silver pin/pendant was copied from a Mexican jewelry design by one of the Indian silversmiths working at the Trading Post in the 1940s. The construction is unusual, indicating it was made by a talented silversmith as a one-of-a-kind piece, possibly commissioned by a customer.

## *Seven*

# TRADER AS ARTIST

One of the least known aspects of Charles Strausenback's life is his career as an artist. Largely self-taught, he began making art as a youth by creating souvenirs from gypsum found in Garden of the Gods.

In his early 20s, he began to draw and paint on paper and canvas; the earliest known paintings date from 1914 and are of cowboys and Western scenes. His subject matter eventually turned to scenes from Garden of the Gods and the Southwest.

He became an accomplished artist, and drawing and painting consumed much of Strausenback's time during the 1930s. Beginning about 1934, many pieces were signed with his pseudonym, Charley Earnesta; this name is derived from his first and middle names, Charles Ernest. It is unknown why he used a different name for some of his artwork.

Before 1935, Strausenback studied briefly under Boardman Robinson, who was director and instructor at the Broadmoor Art Academy before becoming director of the Colorado Springs Fine Arts Center in 1936. Robinson introduced Strausenback to the modernist movement. He began using opaque watercolors to make angular representational paintings of landscapes and Pueblo Indian designs, which were signed Charley Earnesta.

Strausenback's only solo exhibition occurred in 1936, when his modern canvases were displayed in the Chappell House, then the home of the Indian collection of the Denver Art Museum. A critique of the show by art museum director Donald Bear was published in the *Colorado Springs Gazette* on January 8, 1936, under the title, "Strausenback Wins Renown As Artist." In his analysis, Bear wrote:

> Something quite original in picture-making claims our attention when viewing the present show of opaque watercolors by Charley Earnesta now on view at Chappell House. These are neither pictures in the ordinary sense of the word, nor formal designs, having attributes of both. They are picture-designs, suggested by the art of the American Indian, by their painting, their rug designs, and Kachina dolls.
>
> Earnesta, who originated this particular idiom, takes first the natural motif and reworks his material with Indian pattern designs which make the picture. He very wisely insists that these pictures have no symbolic meaning. Because of the gaiety and, likewise, because of their geometry and color, we imagine them as staged sets or as frescoes suited for a simple, functional architecture.
>
> Mr. Earnesta was born in Mexico, is familiar with the art of the Mayan, as well as that of the American Indian, and the native arts and crafts of the southwest. This is an

exhibition that we can enjoy because the work not only fulfills its intention, but is also amusing and not without charm.

While Strausenback exhibited his modern paintings at area art shows, he continued to work in oils and standard watercolor media. Watercolors made in 1936 and 1937, when Charles and Esther began to spend their winters in Phoenix, depict scenes of the Arizona desert, saguaros, the Superstition Mountains, and San Xavier del Bac Mission near Tucson. Oil paintings of this time depict New Mexico adobes and landscapes of the Garden of the Gods. Paintings of this period show a mature artist working in a variety of styles.

Economics may have played a role in Strausenback's next art project. In 1938 and 1939, he produced a series of limited-edition lithographs and etchings encompassing 45 images. Whereas his paintings sold for about $35 each, prints could be sold for the more appealing prices of $7.50 for the smallest subject to $12.50 for the largest of his prints.

The lithographs portray scenes from the Garden of the Gods and Pikes Peak, landscapes of Arizona including the Grand Canyon, Monument Valley, and the Superstition Mountains, New Mexico adobes, and even San Juan Capistrano Mission in California. Cowboy themes reemerged as he made prints of a speeding stagecoach, cowboys on bucking broncs, and western towns. Modern designs were also depicted in his lithographs as Southwestern landscapes. Additionally, Strausenback made portraits of the Navajo and Pueblo Indians who worked for him; Awa Tsireh, Severo Tafoya, and Porfilia Tafoya were among his subjects.

The lithographs were printed in editions ranging from 20 to 50 prints per image. Each lithograph is numbered in the plate in the order it was created. For instance, "Gateway and Pikes Peak" is numbered 1 in the plate, and Strausenback noted in pencil on the bottom of his artist's proof, "1st Litho I ever made Aug 1938."

About the same time as Strausenback produced the lithographs, he also made a small series of etchings with subjects ranging from Navajo and Plains Indians, Garden of the Gods, or the mountains near Phoenix. Five scratchboard images, approximately postcard size and all representing images from the Pikes Peak region, were made in editions of 100 each. These were not signed by Strausenback and were likely sold as souvenirs at budget prices.

Strausenback stopped making art by 1940, as no known examples of his work are dated later than 1939.

Charles Strausenback was largely a self-taught artist. By the 1930s, his subject matter was mainly focused on Garden of the Gods, evidenced by this oil painting of the Gateway Rocks, Cathedral Spires, and Three Graces. (Private collection.)

In the early 1930s, Strausenback studied briefly under Boardman Robinson, director of the Broadmoor Art Academy, who introduced him to the modernist movement. This opaque watercolor painting is Strausenback's modern rendition of the Gateway Rocks in Garden of the Gods with Pikes Peak in the distance. (Private collection.)

Beginning about 1934, many pieces of Charles Strausenback's art were signed Charley Earnesta, as was this modern landscape of Pikes Peak with Zuni heartline deer in the foreground. This pseudonym was derived from his first and middle names. (Private collection.)

Paintings of recognizable American settings, such as Strausenback's lithograph *Painted Desert—Arizona*, encompassed the regional movement by modernists in the 1930s. Whether Strausenback realized it or not, he had joined the debate about modernism and national identity.

Strausenback's modernist paintings were displayed at the Denver Art Museum in 1936 and critiqued by museum director Donald Bear: "These pictures are most entertaining when there is an obvious connection between the natural motif and its formalization. We refer to the patterning of the posteriors of streamlined motors." Bear refers to the painting above, entitled *West Colorado Avenue*, depicting a busy street in Manitou with Pikes Peak looming over the scene. Strausenback also showed this painting at the Colorado Springs Fine Arts Center 21st Annual Exhibition. (Both, private collection.)

PROFESSIONAL MEMBERS

## COLORADO SPRINGS FINE ARTS CENTER

TWENTY-FIRST ANNUAL EXHIBITION

ENTRY SLIP

PRINT TITLE, NAME AND ADDRESS PLAINLY

Title West Colo Ave

Artist Charley Earnesta//

Address P.O. Box 686 Colo Spring

Medium Water color

Price (if for Sale)

Owner (if not for Sale)

Exhibited before? Yes Denver
(if so where?)

35 00 IMPORTANT: FILL OUT AND RETURN TO
COLORADO SPRINGS FINE ARTS CENTER

Strausenback frequently made pencil drawings that were later turned into paintings or lithographs. This drawing of Awa Tsireh is dated 1939 and was copied from a personal photograph of the artist taken by Strausenback. The drawing was later the basis for an oil painting and lithographs. (Garden of the Gods Trading Post.)

Strausenback was fascinated with Pueblo Indian designs and painting techniques. Many of his paintings and even his company logo are reminiscent of Awa Tsireh's artwork, if not direct copies. This 1935 opaque watercolor painting, signed Charley Ernesta, incorporates Pueblo bird and butterfly designs. (Private collection.)

Charles Strausenback depicted the Grand Canyon, as viewed from the South Rim, in two different styles in these lithographs. The print above shows a traditional view of the canyon. To the right is his modern rendition with simplistic flat mesa tops and the Colorado River flowing like a ribbon through the middle of the scene. Both prints were made in 1938.

Once the Strausenbacks began spending the winter months in Phoenix, Charles began using the desert landscapes as subjects for his artwork. These works both depict the Superstition Mountains. Above is a watercolor painting with saguaro cactus, signed Charley Earnesta; below is a 1938 lithograph that was sold from the Strausenback Indian Silver Shops.

In the late 1930s, Charles Strausenback experimented with the medium of copper-plate etchings. The etching above, entitled *Navajos*, depicts two Indians in traditional dress. The subjects are placed in a spatial void in the style typical of American Indian easel art of the early 20th century. Each lithograph or etching Strausenback made was accompanied by a small green-colored paper certificate; the title of the print and the edition was handwritten in pencil by the artist.

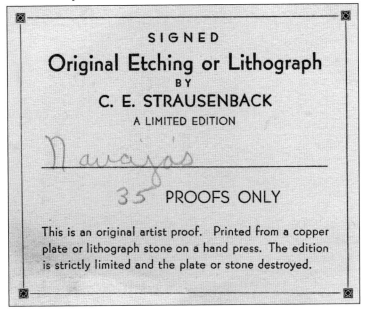

SIGNED
## Original Etching or Lithograph
BY
## C. E. STRAUSENBACK
A LIMITED EDITION

*Navajos*

35 PROOFS ONLY

This is an original artist proof. Printed from a copper plate or lithograph stone on a hand press. The edition is strictly limited and the plate or stone destroyed.

Charles Strausenback displays his sense of humor in this amusing lithograph. Dated 1938, the sixth lithograph he produced shows a car stuck on a mountain peak with the caption, "If this isn't Pikes Peak he's wasted some good driving. Apologies to Frank Owen." The driver is reminiscent of cartoonist Frank Owen's screwball character Jasper.

To accommodate the tourist market accustomed to purchasing postcard souvenirs of their visits to Garden of the Gods, Strausenback produced a series of five scratchboard prints of scenes from the Pikes Peak region that sold at budget prices. Approximately postcard-sized, these prints were made in editions of 100.

# Eight

# SUMMER RESIDENTS

At the turn of the 20th century, the national fascination with Native Americans prompted thousands of Indians to join exhibitions, fairs, Wild West shows, and regional tourist attractions to earn money working as dancers and performers. Dancing offered steady wages plus an opportunity to display their culture and customs in a rewarding manner.

The Indian performers in the Pikes Peak region were dominated by residents of Santa Clara Pueblo. Navajos and other Tewas from New Mexico pueblos danced and worked during the early part of the 20th century, but it was families from Santa Clara who made working in the Indian-themed attractions a family tradition.

The earliest mention of Santa Clara Indians entertaining in the Pikes Peak region is in 1898, when they were invited to Colorado Springs to participate in the sixth annual Flower Carnival. Approximately 30 members of the pueblo were accompanied by the government school teacher and agent. They camped at the Broadmoor Casino and performed four of their traditional dances for a large crowd. A *Colorado Springs Gazette* article on September 2, 1898, stated, "After the dances yesterday the Indians sold articles of pottery and pipes, etc. to the onlookers. They disposed of quite a considerable amount of stuff."

For the Santa Claras, this trip served as a significant source of income for a community struggling with the rapid change from subsistence farming to a cash economy. In a November 28, 1900, *Colorado Springs Gazette* article titled "A Pueblo's Grievance," Alvino Chavarria described the economic conditions of the Pueblo:

Before the white men came into New Mexico the Santa Claras were a rich, prosperous and peaceful people, cultivating their farms on the banks of the Rio Grande with comprehensive irrigation systems. They had large herds of cattle, sheep, and goats, and it was never thought when allotments of money were made to the other Indian tribes that the Santa Claras would need government bounty. But in the last few years the extension of irrigation enterprises in the upper valley of the Rio Grande, in Colorado, has left the lower course dry. There is only a waste of dry sand in front of the headgates of the Indians' ditches, and they have been reduced to poverty. A few of the Santa Claras still cultivate small gardens and vineyards with water drawn from wells, and a few keep small flocks on the scanty desert herbage, but most of them are earning a hard living on the railroads and ranches and ditches of the white man.

Performing at tourist venues was good seasonal employment at a time when Indians did not have many opportunities off the reservations. One other way for Southwestern Indians to earn an income was to work as silversmiths. Merchants recognized that the presence of an Indian silversmith practicing his trade in view of the customers boosted their sales of Indian jewelry. Therefore, many Navajo and Pueblo silversmiths left home, either on a seasonal or permanent basis, to work in curio stores from Hollywood to New York or at tourist venues such as Garden of the Gods.

However, leaving the reservation for extended periods to work outside of the area until the mid-1920s was no easy task. Travel rights were restricted for American Indians until the passage of the Indian Citizen Act in 1924, which granted citizenship to all Natives born in the United States. Before then, Indians were considered wards of the federal government, and were required to obtain a pass from the government agent before lawfully leaving reservations.

Travel from northern New Mexico to Colorado Springs was made easier in the late 1880s, when the Denver & Rio Grande Railroad completed a branch to Santa Fe. The tracks were laid through Española and near Santa Clara Pueblo. This allowed three generations of the Silva/Tafoya family to work in the Pikes Peak region for decades.

Most of the advertising images of the Indians working in the Pikes Peak area show them adorned with Plains-style feathered headdresses. By the early 20th century, the prevailing image of Native authenticity was that of the Plains Indian, largely based on the stereotypes propagated in the Wild West shows traveling the United States and Europe. These stereotypes were perpetuated in tourist venues across the country well into the 20th century with Indian performers of any tribal heritage dressed in Plains-style attire. But the use of a Plains-style feathered headdress was customary for the Tewas of the northern Pueblos, as they had developed their own style of eagle feather headdresses for formal and ceremonial use long before encountering American tourists. Their adoption of a Plains headdress is attributable to their historic interactions with the southern Plains tribes who roamed in northern New Mexico.

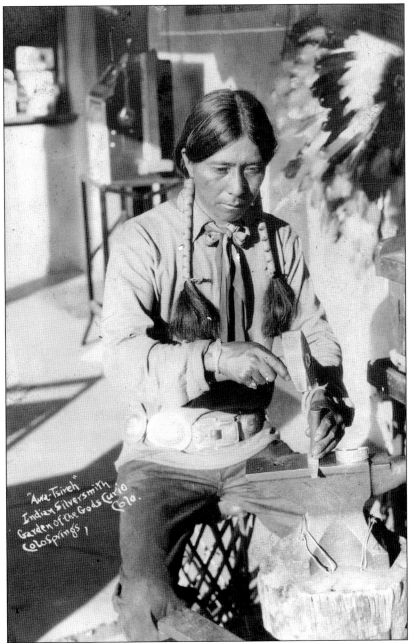

"Awa Tsireh"
Indian Silversmith
Garden of the Gods Curio
Colo Springs 1
Colo.

The most celebrated silversmith to work at the Trading Post was Awa Tsireh (Alfonso Roybal), born in San Ildefonso Pueblo in 1898. It is not known when or from whom Awa Tsireh learned silversmithing, but by 1931, he was described in newspaper articles as a painter, a silversmith, and a dancer. Awa Tsireh's association with Charles Strausenback had begun by 1930, and his younger brother, Ralph Roybal (Ma Wholo Peen) also worked as a silversmith at the Trading Post in 1938. Awa Tsireh was employed by Strausenback for nearly two decades; his sister once stated that during the summer months in the 1930s and 1940s, he used to go to a shop in Colorado Springs and do his paintings and silverwork there. Awa Tsireh considered Strausenback a friend and sometimes traveled to Florida with him in the summer.

The only known lithograph produced by Awa Tsireh was done at the Trading Post in the late 1930s. Titled *Owl and Skunks*, it was published in a series of only 25 prints and sold for $10. Skunks were a popular subject for Awa Tsireh, as he also produced a number of silver skunk pins while working for Strausenback. (Above, Garden of the Gods Trading Post.)

On June 26, 1938, the Hutchinson, Kansas, *News-Herald* reported on the impending nuptials of a local couple, exclaiming, "Spell it Awa Tsireh—pronounce is A-Wa Si-dy! Whoever he is, he's the Indian silversmith responsible for that symbolical silver plate which Elizabeth and Joe, to wed today, will give choice place in their household. Of about luncheon size, the plate center is beaten and etched with a god to watch over them, and filled in about and on the rim with emblems of wisdom, constancy, love and happiness. There is no other plate like it and there won't be for the famous 'Awa Sidy' never duplicates. Of New Mexico originally, he's now collaborating with Charles E. Strausenback in a museum at the Garden of the Gods." This tray, similar to the one given as a wedding gift to Elizabeth and Joe, was made by Awa Tsireh from aluminum, a metal that was occasionally used by Indian silversmiths at the Trading Post.

The photograph to the left was taken by Charles Strausenback while Awa Tsireh worked with him at the Trading Post in the 1930s. It was the basis for a pencil sketch made by Strausenback in 1939, as well as a series of lithographs. The lithographs were printed in two different versions: monotone and sepia-toned. The print below is No. 14 from the sepia-toned series. (Left, Garden of the Gods Trading Post.)

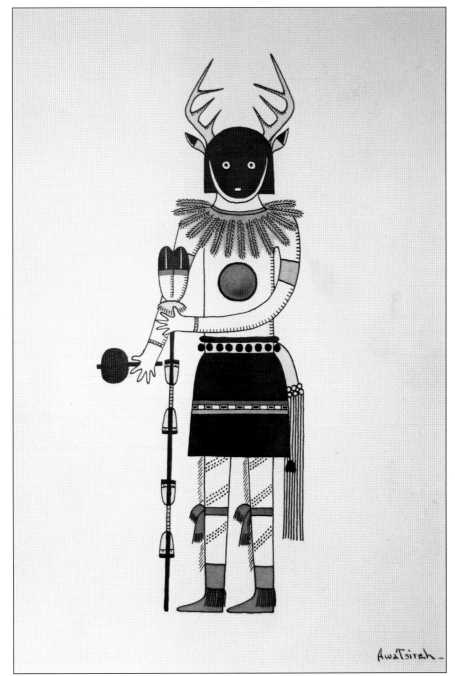

Awa Tsireh painted this modernist watercolor of a deer dancer around 1925. As a boy, he made sketches even before attending San Ildefonso Day School, but he did not continue his education, and his art skills were mostly self-taught. About 1920, Awa Tsireh married a woman from the village; the following year she gave birth to a son, but mother and child died soon thereafter. This loss affected the artist greatly, and he moved back to his parents' home where he took solace in his artwork and never remarried. He gained fame as an easel artist in the 1920s with a show in Chicago. By the 1930s, his paintings had become increasingly sought after.

Awa Tsireh's association with Charles Strausenback may have ended in the early 1940s, possibly during World War II. It is not known if he continued to work as a silversmith after leaving the Trading Post, but his production of paintings diminished. Though he traveled fairly often, especially in summer, he always made San Ildefonso Pueblo his home. Awa Tsireh passed away on March 29, 1955. He was remembered as a quiet man, with a good sense of humor. His paintings were meticulously and precisely drawn in both realistic and abstract styles of Pueblo themes and mythology, including animals and black-and-white striped sacred clowns.

Sotero Montoya, born at San Ildefonso Pueblo in 1898, was also known as Charles Montoya. He learned silversmithing at the Trading Post and worked for Charles Strausenback as a silversmith and an easel artist, signing his paintings with his Tewa name, O-Qo-Wa-Mo-Nu. Anthropologist John Adair wrote in his field notes (housed at Wheelwright Museum in Santa Fe, New Mexico) on May 22, 1940, "I talked with Charley Mantayeh [sic]. He says that he makes silver. He learned in the shop of Strassenburg [sic] at the Garden of the Gods, in Colo. Springs. He is engaged in making it just in the summer when he goes up to that shop in the summer. He also has gone to Miami Florida in the winter with Strassenburg, and made it there as well."

Hoske Nal Wooty was born about 1890 on the Navajo reservation and changed his name to William Goodluck while attending Carlisle Indian School from 1909 to 1912. Though he likely learned to work silver from his father, he is first identified as a silversmith in 1914 when he was working in Manuelito, New Mexico. He was employed by Charles Strausenback as a silversmith at the Indian (above) and identified on souvenir postcards as Host-Nat-Woty. Goodluck brought his family to Colorado Springs where his wife Yekanasbah worked as a rug weaver. Goodluck followed Strausenback to the Trading Post in 1929 (below), where his father, the renowned silversmith Hosteen Goodluck, joined him. William worked silver for many decades, attaining a reputation as a master silversmith often referred to as "Billie Goodluck." When not in Colorado, he worked from his home in Arizona, where he died in October 1967.

John Etsitty, Navajo, shown here working as a silversmith at Zion National Park during the 1930s, preferred to be called John or Johnny Silversmith. He may have been born around 1905 in the Ganado, Arizona, area. He worked as a silversmith for Charles Strausenback in the late 1930s and early 1940s, in the winters at the Hotel Adams Gift Shop in Phoenix and at the Trading Post during the summers.

Juan Jose Gutierrez served as governor of Santa Clara Pueblo in 1905, when Edward S. Curtis photographed him for *The North American Indian* series of books. Curtis identified him as "Oyegi-aye" translated as "Frost Moving." Gutierrez worked for Charles Strausenback as an entertainer and weaver at the Indian from 1924 until 1928, but he never worked at the Trading Post. Gutierrez was frequently photographed by Strausenback for advertising postcards and identified as "O-Yegy-On't-Ya" or "Frost at Sunrise." The postcards proclaimed Gutierrez was born in 1838, but his birthdate was actually around 1856. Gutierrez died at Santa Clara Pueblo in the early 1930s.

Epifanio Tafoya, or Na-Na-Ping, was the first silversmith to work for Charles Strausenback at Garden of the Gods Curio Company in 1920. Born in Santa Clara Pueblo about 1879, Epifanio was photographed working silver at Manitou Cliff Dwellings in 1924 by Horace S. Poley. He was then photographed at the Indian working for Strausenback around 1925. Epifanio died August 26, 1933.

Pueblo Indian "na-na-ping"    Colo. Springs, Colo.
Garden Of the Gods Curio Co.

Indian Silversmith "Ca-Ping" Colo-Springs Colo.
Garden of the Gods Curio Co

Severo Tafoya, whose Tewa name was Ca-Ping, or "Quaking Aspen," was born in either 1904 or 1906 at Santa Clara Pueblo. He came to Colorado Springs around 1925 with his uncle Epifanio Tafoya, from whom he learned silversmithing. Severo hired on with Charles Strausenback to work at the Indian, where he and his wife, Ja-Ro, lived year-round in a Navajo hogan.

Severo Tafoya, or Ca-Ping, worked as a silversmith for Charles Strausenback for decades. Here he is seen on the porch of the Trading Post. Severo spoke English, Spanish, and Tewa, and in his youth attended Santa Fe Indian School.

Severo (Ca-Ping) and Porfilia (Ja-Ro) Tafoya were married in Manitou on September 13, 1925. The Tafoyas made a permanent home in Colorado Springs, where Severo died in 1985, preceded in death by Porfilia. Through the years, they also worked at Seven Falls, Cave of the Winds, the Iron Springs Chateau, the Hidden Inn, and the Broadmoor.

Antonio Silva was born at Santa Clara Pueblo in 1879. His Tewa name was Tsidi P'i', which means "Red Bird," but it was phonetically spelled Seda-Pee or Cherepee. His wife passed away shortly after their daughter Agapita was born in 1904, and he became a single father. By 1915, he began working seasonally in the Pikes Peak region and was photographed near Balanced Rock with his family, indicating his first employer may have been Curt Goerke. He worked for Charles Strausenback off and on before being employed in the 1920s as an entertainer at the Hidden Inn, where he posed for photographs with tourists until he retired in 1948. It is unknown why Antonio Silva was always identified as either Joe or Jose Tafoya.

Agapita Silva was born at Santa Clara Pueblo in 1904; by the 1920s, she was working as a potter. She married Camilio "Sunflower" Tafoya (Bo-Be-Tsá-A-Inyah) in 1931. He was born at the pueblo in 1902 and was one of the first-known male potters in Santa Clara. Husbands and wives in Pueblo pottery families typically collaborated, as did Camilio and Agapita, who made black and red carved wares. After the death of Agapita in 1959, Camilio became famous in the 1960s for developing, with his children Joseph Lonewolf and Grace Medicine Flower, a style of miniature pottery with beautifully carved designs. Camilio passed away in 1995. (Left, Garden of the Gods Trading Post.)

The Tafoya family of Santa Clara Pueblo danced at the Trading Post from 1946 to 1947 before going over to the Hidden Inn in 1948. From left to right are Joe Louis, Agapita, Camilio, and Mary Grace. Joe Louis was born in 1935, and Mary Grace (Grace Medicine Flower) in 1938.

Vidal Silva, Na-Na-Tse, was born to Agapita Silva in 1928 at Santa Clara Pueblo. Vidal's father died, and he was adopted by his stepfather Camilio Tafoya. He first came to Garden of the Gods with his parents in the 1930s. After serving in the Korean War, he changed his name to Vidal S. Cloudeagle and returned to Manitou to participate in the family business of native dancing. He died in 2014.

Severiano Naranjo, whose Tewa name was Don Ying'ye, was born about 1885 in Santa Clara Pueblo, a nephew of Epifanio Tafoya. Severiano married Clarita Naranjo, or Pobe Senge, and they brought their family to Garden of the Gods to work at the Indian in the mid-1920s. His youngest son was featured in Charles Strausenback's advertising postcards identified by his Tewa name, Wha-Be. In the above photograph, the family stands in front of Balanced Rock about 1926.

# BIBLIOGRAPHY

Adair, John. *The Navajo and Pueblo Silversmiths.* Norman, OK: University of Oklahoma Press, 1944.

Gehling, Richard, and Mary Ann Gehling. *Man in the Garden of the Gods.* 2nd Edition. Woodland Park, CO: Mountain Automation Corporation, 1998.

Hamill, Toni, and the Manitou Springs Heritage Center. *Images of America: Garden of the Gods.* Charleston, SC: Arcadia Publishing, 2012.

Harrison, Deborah. *Images of America: Manitou Springs.* Charleston, SC: Arcadia Publishing, 2003.

Higdon, Myrl. *The History of Garden of the Gods.* Kelly Kilgore Chilcott Collection, Billie Jane Baguley Library and Archives, RC366(3):2.1–2.3. Phoenix, AZ: Heard Museum, 1996.

Hill, W.W. *An Ethnography of Santa Clara Pueblo, New Mexico.* Edited by Charles H. Lange. Albuquerque, NM: University of New Mexico Press, 1982.

Messier, Pat, and Kim Messier. *Reassessing Hallmarks of Native Southwest Jewelry: Artists, Traders, Guilds and the Government.* Atglen, PA: Schiffer Publishing, 2014.

Pardue, Diana F., and Norman L. Sandfield. *Awa Tsireh: Pueblo Painter and Metalsmith.* Phoenix, AZ: Heard Museum, 2017.

Seymour, Tryntje Van Ness. *When the Rainbow Touches Down.* Phoenix, AZ: Heard Museum, 1988.

# DISCOVER THOUSANDS OF LOCAL HISTORY BOOKS
## FEATURING MILLIONS OF VINTAGE IMAGES

Arcadia Publishing, the leading local history publisher in the United States, is committed to making history accessible and meaningful through publishing books that celebrate and preserve the heritage of America's people and places.

## Find more books like this at
## www.arcadiapublishing.com

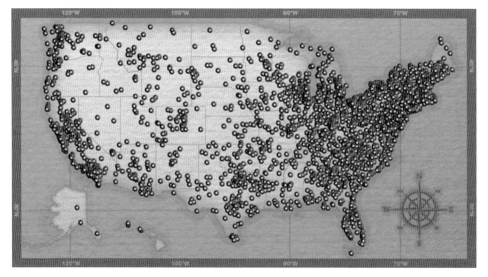

Search for your hometown history, your old stomping grounds, and even your favorite sports team.

Consistent with our mission to preserve history on a local level, this book was printed in South Carolina on American-made paper and manufactured entirely in the United States. Products carrying the accredited Forest Stewardship Council (FSC) label are printed on 100 percent FSC-certified paper.

**MADE IN THE**
**USA**